Ninja Dual Zone
Air Fryer Cookbook
for Beginners UK

Effortless and Flavorful Ninja Air Fryer Meals for Your
Whole Family to Fry, Bake, Broil, Grill, Roast, Reheat
and Dehydrate

Matt A. Diedrich

Contents

Introduction *1*

Getting to know the Ninja Dual Zone......... 1

So, What is the Ninja Dual Zone Air Fryer? 1

Why Choose the Ninja Dual Zone? 2

The Benefits of the Ninja Dual Zone Air Fryer2

How to Clean the Ninja Dual Zone Air Fryer? 3

Possible Risks 3

Tips and Tricks to Using the Ninja Dual Zone

Air Fryer 4

FAQs 5

Chapter 1: Breakfast Recipes *6*

Avocado Egg Boats............................. 6

Baked Oatmeal Bites 6

Broiled Grapefruit 6

Dehydrated Fruit and Nut Granola 7

Dehydrated Yoghurt Drops 7

Breakfast Bruschetta 7

Baked Breakfast Quiche 8

Granola Bars 8

Breakfast Scones............................... 8

Breakfast Tacos 9

Breakfast Avocado Bread 9

Breakfast Hash Browns 10

Apple and custard crumble rolls 10

Flapjacks with Strawberry Jam 10

Simple Breakfast Muffins 11

Brown Sugar & Pecan Air Fryer Apples...... 11

French Toast Cups with Raspberries: 11

Apple Pie Egg Roll 12

Double Cherry Mini Egg Rolls 12

Bacon Omelette 13

Tropical French toast 13

Crispy Bacon Breakfast Muffin 13

Maple Cinnamon Oatmeal Breakfast Cookies

.... 14

Air Fried Egg & Crispy Honey Bacon 14

Chapter 2: Main Courses *15*

Chimichangas 15

Chicken Cordon Bleu 15

Korean Fried Chicken......................... 16

Salmon Teriyaki 16

Tandoori Chicken Thighs 17

Sesame-Ginger Beef Skewers.................. 18

Baked Cajun Shrimp and Sausage Foil Packets

.... 18

Roasted Turkey Breast with Cranberry Glaze 19

Blackened Mahi-Mahi Tacos 19

Panko-Crusted Salmon with Honey-Mustard

Glaze 20

Vegetable and Chickpea Fritters 21

Tofu Banh Mi Sandwiches 21

Vegan Falafel 22

Butternut Squash and Black Bean Tacos ... 22

Vegan Meatballs made with Lentils and

Vegetables 23

Stuffed Peppers with Rice, Beans and

Vegetables 23

Dehydrated Air Fryer Beef Jerky 24

Fried Black Pudding 24

Baked Honey Mustard Salmon Fillets in the Air

Fryer 25

Broiled Lobster Tails with Lemon Butter Sauce

.... 25

Chapter 3: Fish and Seafood............ 26
Seafood Paella.............................26
Shrimp and Scallop Skewers with Chimichurri Sauce 26
Sesame-Crusted Ahi Tuna 27
Spicy Cajun Catfish.........................27
Beer-Battered Fish Tacos 27
Coconut-Crusted Mahi-Mahi 28
Lobster Mac and Cheese Bites 28
Salmon Croquettes with Lemon-Dill Sauce 29
Shrimp Scampi with Linguine 29
Tandoori Shrimp Skewers 30
Crab Stuffed Mushrooms 30
Lobster Ravioli with Brown Butter Sauce ...31
Cajun Garlic Butter Shrimp 31
Baked Thai Fish Cakes with Sweet Chili Sauce 31
Blackened Red Snapper with Mango Salsa 32

Chapter 4: Poultry & Meat Recipes ... 33
Szechuan Pepper Steak 33
Chicken Liver Pate 33
Braised Lamb Shanks 34
Fried Pig Ears 34
Rosemary and Garlic Pork Tenderloin 35
BBQ Pulled Pork Sliders 35
Nashville Hot Chicken Sandwiches 36
Dehydrated Venison Jerky 36
Buffalo Turkey Meatballs 37
Baked Pesto-Stuffed Chicken Breasts........37
Baked Bone Marrow 38
Smoky Chipotle Beef Ribs 38
Spicy Korean Pork Belly 39
Tandoori Chicken Skewers 39
Thai Basil Chicken Stir-Fry 39

Vietnamese Grilled Lemongrass Pork Chops 40
Jamaican Jerk Pork Tenderloin with Pineapple Salsa 41
Moroccan-Spiced Chicken Thighs with Apricot Chutney 41

Chapter 5: Healthy Vegetables and Sides 42
Broiled Asparagus with Lemon and Parmesan 42
Dehydrated Vegetable Chips with Sea Salt...42
Broiled Brussel Sprouts with Balsamic Glaze42
Broiled Eggplant with Garlic and Tahini Sauce 43
Crispy Brussel Sprouts with Maple Glaze ...43
Zucchini Fries with Garlic Aioli 44
Vegan Spring Rolls with Peanut Dipping Sauce 44
Baked Sweet Potatoes with Sage and Walnuts 45
Crispy Kale Chips with Smoked Paprika ...45
Butternut Squash Risotto Cakes 45
Stuffed Artichokes with Parmesan and Herbs 46
Vegan Falafel Patties 47
Herbed Hasselback Potatoes 47
Parmesan-Roasted Asparagus 48
Turmeric-Roasted Chickpeas 48
Miso-Glazed Eggplant 48
Stuffed Acorn Squash with Wild Rice and Mushrooms 49
Spicy Baked Sweet Potato Wedges............49

Chapter 6: Fast and Easy Everyday Favourites 50
Quails Eggs in Yorkshire Puddings............50

Crispy Parmesan Chicken Tenders 50

Vegetarian Quesadillas with Avocado Cream 50

Cheesy Beef Empanadas........................ 51

Spinach and Feta Stuffed Chicken Breasts ... 52

Cajun Fish Tacos with Cilantro Lime Sauce 52

Pork Carnitas Bowls with Avocado and Lime 53

Buffalo Cauliflower Wings with Blue Cheese

Dip 53

Vietnamese Pork and Vermicelli Bowls 54

Baked Panko-Crusted Crab Cakes 55

Chicken Fajitas with Bell Peppers and Onions

.... 55

Hawaiian Teriyaki Chicken Skewers with

Pineapple Salsa 56

Indian Butter Chicken with Naan Bread...... 56

Sesame-Ginger Tofu Bowls with Bok Choy and

Shiitake Mushrooms 57

Mushroom Risotto Balls 58

Chapter 7: Holiday Specials *59*

Maple-Glazed Ham with Bourbon and Brown

Sugar 59

Turducken Roulade with Cranberry Stuffing 59

Christmas Pudding 60

Sweet Potato Casserole with Pecan Streusel

Topping 60

Balsamic Glazed Roasted Root Vegetables   61

Cornish Game Hens with Herb and Citrus

Stuffing 62

Sage and Sausage Stuffing Balls.............. 62

Spiced Cranberry Glazed Pork Tenderloin ... 63

Eggnog French Toast with Cinnamon Whipped

Cream 63

Rosemary and Garlic Leg of Lamb with Red

Wine Sauce 64

Gingerbread Cake with Cream Cheese Frosting

.... 64

Candied Yams with Marshmallows and Pecans

.... 65

Chapter 8: Snacks and Desserts *66*

Beignets 66

Cinnamon Sugar Doughnut Holes 66

Roasted Beet Chips with Feta Cheese Dip ... 67

Salted Caramel Popcorn 67

S'mores Empanadas with Marshmallow Filling

.... 67

Chocolate and Peanut Butter Stuffed Dates   68

Savory Parmesan Churros with Herb Dip ... 68

Caramelised Banana Bread Pudding 69

Sweet Potato Fries with Cinnamon Sugar and

Nutmeg 69

Lemon-Poppy Seed Scones.................... 70

Mini Cherry Pies with Vanilla Bean Ice Cream

.... 70

Cinnamon and Sugar Fried Wontons with

Vanilla Cream Dip 71

Chocolate Lava Cakes with Raspberry Coulis

.... 71

Caramelized Onion and Gruyere Tartlets ... 72

Churro Bites with Dulce de Leche Dip 73

Cheesy Broccoli Bites......................... 73

Chapter 9: Staples, Sauces, Dips, and

Dressings *74*

Baked Garlic and Herb Croutons 74

Caramelized Watermelon Cubes.............. 74

Roasted Garlic Hummus....................... 74

Jalapeño-Cilantro Hummus 75

Sun-Dried Tomato Tapenade 75

Crispy Tofu Bites 76

Baked Zucchini Blooms 76

Fruit Leathers 77

Mushroom Jerky 77

Spaghetti Nests 78

Stuffed Mushrooms with Sausage and Cheese
.... 78

Baked Ziti with Tomato Sauce and Mozzarella
Cheese 78

Stuffed Peppers with Rice and Ground Beef 79

Jalapeno Poppers with Spicy Mayo Dip 79

Corn on the Cob with Herb Butter 80

Buffalo Cauliflower Bites with Blue Cheese
Dip 80

Pita Chips with Za'atar and Olive Oil........ 81

Cinnamon Sugar Pretzel Bites with Cream

Cheese Dip 81

Chapter 10: Desserts 82

Mini Sticky Toffee Puddings 82

Brownie Bites with Peanut Butter Frosting   82

Peach Cobbler 83

Mixed Berry Cupcakes 83

Pumpkin Pie 84

Bread And Butter Pudding 84

Scottish Smoked Salmon Bake 85

Traditional Steak and Kidney Pie 85

Zesty Lemon Cake Pots 86

Fruit Bake Duo 86

Sweet & Sour Chicken Balls 87

Easy Cinnamon Pear Cake 87

Introduction

Cooking has always been an important part of my life, starting from a young age when I would eagerly assist my mother in the kitchen as we baked simple treats like fairy cakes, brownies, and flapjacks. The joy of creating something delicious from scratch and the satisfaction of sharing it with family and friends has always been a source of happiness for me. As I grew up, my interest in cooking only intensified, and I began exploring new ingredients and flavours, taking inspiration from different cultures and cuisines.

Moving across countries with my own small family only served to further fuel my passion for cooking. I found myself excited by the prospect of discovering new ingredients and cooking techniques that were unique to the places we lived in. And with each move, my culinary horizons expanded, as I incorporated new ingredients into my recipes, creating dishes that reflected the flavours and cultures of the places we had lived in.

During the COVID-19 lockdown, like many others, my family and I were looking for ways to stay healthy and reduce our intake of oily, fried foods. That's when we decided to invest in an air fryer, and it was a game-changer. The air fryer allowed us to create crispy, delicious foods that tasted like they were deep-fried, but with a fraction of the oil. We were able to cook everything from chicken wings to French fries, all without the mess and fuss that comes with traditional frying.

As we explored the potential of our air fryer, we realised that it had much more to offer than just healthy fried foods. We began experimenting with sweet and savoury recipes, creating dishes that were not only delicious but also easy to make. And that's when I decided to start creating my recipe book.

My air fryer cookbook is designed specifically for the Ninja Dual Zone air fryer, with adjusted cooking times and temperatures for the best results. Each recipe has been lovingly tried and tested by myself and my wonderful mother, ensuring that they are simple, delicious, and require minimal dishes.

From breakfast to dinner, snacks to desserts, I have included a wide range of recipes for you to explore and enjoy. Whether you're looking for a quick and easy meal or an impressive dinner party dish, my air fryer cookbook has got you covered. And the best part? You can create all these dishes with just one appliance, without the need for multiple pots and pans.

So, whether you're a seasoned cook or a novice in the kitchen, I invite you to join me on this exciting culinary journey with the Ninja Dual Zone air fryer. With this handy appliance and my delicious recipes, you'll be cooking up a storm in no time. Let's explore the world of air frying together, and discover all the amazing dishes we can create!

Getting to know the Ninja Dual Zone

If you've recently bought the Ninja Dual Zone air fryer, you may be feeling a little overwhelmed and unsure of how to use it. However, fear not, as I am here to guide you through everything you need to know. Despite their initial complexity, air fryers are actually incredibly easy to use, with a simplicity akin to that of a standard microwave. So, let's get started on this exciting new cooking journey together!

So, What is the Ninja Dual Zone Air Fryer?

Unlike other air fryers, the Ninja Dual Zone offers a unique cooking experience thanks to its two separate cooking areas, which can be set at different temperatures and settings. This exceptional feature allows you to simultaneously prepare a main course and a side dish, both of which will finish cooking at the exact same time! If you're someone who loves hosting dinner parties, the Ninja Dual Zone is an absolute game-changer, as it frees up your time to mingle with your guests while it does all the hard work.

Moreover, the Ninja Dual Zone has preset modes that cater to various cooking styles such as max crisp, roast, bake, reheat, dehydrate, and air fry. These modes enable even the most inexperienced cooks to breeze through meal preparation without worrying about temperatures or constantly checking their food through a greasy oven window. In this recipe book, I have included a special holiday chapter that showcases the Ninja Dual Zone's impressive capabilities as a Christmas lifesaver. With this versatile kitchen appliance, you can easily warm up mince pies alongside your turkey, mull wine while you prepare your starters, or even have dessert cooking right next to your main meal. The options are truly endless, and I highly recommend that you experiment with the features of the Ninja Dual Zone by cooking the main meal alongside your sides using my carefully crafted recipes. So, let's get cooking and explore the incredible potential of the Ninja Dual Zone air fryer!

Why Choose the Ninja Dual Zone?

Air fryers have taken the world by storm and it's easy to feel overwhelmed when trying to choose the right one for your kitchen. With so many different brands and models, it's important to find one that suits your specific needs. The Ninja Dual Zone, however, stands out from the rest with its unique feature of having two separate cooking areas that can cook different meals at different temperatures simultaneously. This is especially useful for families with picky eaters or those who love entertaining guests with different dietary requirements.

But the Ninja Dual Zone isn't just about convenience, it also offers a wide range of accessories to enhance your cooking experience.

You can easily bake cakes, pizzas, and more with the various accessories available from the Ninja store. Plus, the ease of clean-up after cooking a multi-course meal is simply amazing!

If you're looking to invest in an air fryer, the Ninja Dual Zone is definitely worth considering. Its flexibility and versatility make it a must-have in any kitchen. And with the added bonus of this recipe book, you can now take your air frying skills to the next level and impress your family and friends with delicious and healthy meals! So what are you waiting for? Get your hands on the Ninja Dual Zone and start cooking up a storm!

The Benefits of the Ninja Dual Zone Air Fryer

In today's world, efficiency and cost-effectiveness are major concerns, especially when it comes to using electrical appliances. With the Ninja Dual Zone air fryer, you can enjoy the benefit of cooking food 75% faster than with a conventional oven, resulting in significantly reduced electricity consumption. I was pleasantly surprised by the amount of money my family saved on electricity bills after using the Ninja Dual Zone to cook a full roast dinner, which would have required much more energy if prepared using a traditional oven. Whether it's for large family meals, holiday gatherings, or birthday parties, the Ninja Dual Zone has been a lifesaver in terms of saving energy and reducing costs.

The Ninja Dual Zone's impressive 7.5L capacity is another benefit that sets it apart from other air fryers. I was surprised at just how much food I could cook in a single batch, which is a tremendous time saver when compared to cooking in multiple batches, as required with other brands of air fryers. The two separate cooking zones have also been a game-changer for me, as I no longer need to use multiple appliances to prepare a meal. With the Ninja Dual Zone, I can cook multiple dishes at different temperatures and times, all within the same appliance, without worrying about timing or juggling different pots and pans. This leaves me with more time to entertain guests and enjoy their company while the Ninja Dual Zone does all the hard work.

The health benefits of the Ninja Dual Zone are also worth mentioning. With its ability to cook food using 75% less fat than traditional cooking methods, it has been a lifesaver for me, especially during lockdown when outdoor activities were limited. I can now prepare my family's favourite fried foods, such as chips or pasta crisps, with very little oil, resulting in a healthier, guilt-free snack.

Overall, I highly recommend the Ninja Dual Zone air fryer to anyone looking for a cost-effective and energy-efficient way to prepare delicious, healthy meals quickly and easily. With the added bonus of being able to create an array of mouth-watering recipes using my Ninja Dual Zone, it's no wonder I find myself recommending it to others all the time.

How to Clean the Ninja Dual Zone Air Fryer?

If you're anything like me, the thought of cleaning up a mountain of greasy dishes after cooking a meal can be incredibly discouraging. As much as I enjoy cooking, the tedious task of scrubbing casserole dishes and pans can take away the joy of the experience. That's why the Ninja Dual Zone is a game-changer when it comes to cleaning up after cooking.

The compartments of the Ninja Dual Zone are designed with non-stick surfaces that make cleaning a breeze. In addition, they are dishwasher safe, which makes the cleaning process even easier! Most of the recipes in this cookbook suggest using a non-stick cooking spray or lining the trays with baking paper to reduce mess and make clean-up even easier.

To clean the Ninja Dual Zone, I recommend washing it by hand using hot soapy water and a sponge. Alternatively, you can rinse out the parts and place them in your dishwasher for even more convenience. One of the best things about the Ninja Dual Zone is that you can safely use baking paper or aluminium foil during cooking, which saves even more time when it comes to cleaning up. Other air fryer brands may not allow the use of baking paper or aluminium foil, so this is a huge plus for the Ninja Dual Zone.

For those stubborn, burnt-on messes, Ninja also offers a handy cleaning brush that can help remove even the toughest grime. We recommend using hot soapy water along with the Ninja cleaning brush for the best results.

In addition, there are tray liners that you can purchase, some of which are specifically designed for the Ninja Dual Zone. These liners are a great option that not only makes clean-up even easier but also reduces the need for baking paper or aluminium foil, which is more environmentally friendly.

The Ninja Dual Zone air fryer makes cleaning up after cooking a breeze. You'll no longer have to dread the thought of cleaning up after a delicious meal. With the Ninja Dual Zone, you can enjoy your cooking experience and leave the cleaning worries behind.

Possible Risks

One significant concern that I have come across while utilising my Ninja Dual Zone air fryer, as well as other air fryer brands, is the rapid increase in temperature. If the food being prepared is not monitored regularly, there is a possibility that it could burn. To mitigate this risk, it is recommended to utilise tried-and-tested recipes and keep a close eye on any new dishes being made using an air fryer.

It is also important to note that air frying, or any frying process, typically requires high temperatures, which has led to discussions of cancer risks. While there is no concrete evidence linking air-fried food to cancer, the cooking of certain foods at high temperatures can lead to the production of cholesterol oxidation products (COPs), which are not beneficial to the human body. Despite this, there is no direct correlation between air frying foods or using the Ninja Dual Zone air fryer and the formation of COPs. Like anything else, there are potential risks, and until scientific evidence suggests otherwise, I will continue to enjoy using my air fryer.

Tips and Tricks to Using the Ninja Dual Zone Air Fryer

The Ninja Dual Zone air fryer is a versatile cooking appliance that can make meal preparation quick and easy. To get the most out of your air fryer, consider investing in some accessories such as silicone oven mitts and racks, which can enhance your cooking experience. You can find these and other helpful accessories on the Ninja store online or at other air fryer shops.

In addition to using accessories, there are some tips that can help you achieve optimal cooking results with your air fryer. One such tip is to line the trays with parchment paper or foil to make cleaning up after cooking a breeze. Weighing your food before cooking can also help you program your air fryer more accurately, resulting in better cooking results.

It is important to note that overfilling the drawers of your Ninja Dual Zone can cause problems, such as the drawers not closing properly. However, the drawers can contain a lot of food, which allows you to cook large meals in one go. To prevent messes, it is recommended to press breadcrumbs firmly onto food when breading, and to flip or shake food halfway through cooking for even results.

Preheating the air fryer can also lead to more even cooking, especially for baked items. And while the air fryer does use less oil than traditional frying methods, it is important to follow recipe instructions regarding the amount of oil to use, as adding too much oil can result in greasy, oily food that is difficult to clean up. With these tips in mind, you can make the most out of your Ninja Dual Zone air fryer and enjoy delicious meals with less mess and hassle.

Here are some additional tips and tricks for using the Ninja Dual Zone air fryer:

- **Use the right temperature and time settings**: Different foods require different cooking temperatures and times. It's essential to follow the instructions in your recipe book or online guides to ensure that your food is cooked to perfection. For instance, frozen foods need higher temperatures and longer cooking times, while fresh ingredients may require lower temperatures and shorter cooking times. Always refer to the instructions for the recommended settings for your specific food.
- **Don't overcrowd the drawers**: While the Ninja Dual Zone has large drawers, it's still important not to overfill them. Overcrowding can lead to uneven cooking, which means that some parts of the food will be overcooked, while others will be undercooked. The solution is to cook in smaller batches or use the racks provided with your air fryer. Using the racks allows you to cook more food at once without overcrowding the drawers.
- **Use the right accessories:** The Ninja Dual Zone comes with a range of accessories, including racks, silicone mitts, and other tools. Make sure to use these accessories correctly to get the best results. For example, use the racks to cook multiple items at once, the silicone mitts to handle hot trays and pans, and other tools to make your cooking experience more comfortable and convenient.
- **Clean your air fryer regularly:** To ensure that your air fryer is always in top condition, you need to clean it after each use. The good news is that the Ninja Dual Zone is easy to clean, thanks to its non-stick surfaces. You can simply wipe it down with a damp cloth or sponge after use. It's also recommended that you clean the accessories that come with your air fryer, such as the racks and silicone mitts, to keep them in good condition.
- **Experiment with different recipes:** The Ninja Dual Zone air fryer is a versatile kitchen appliance that can cook a wide variety of

dishes. Don't be afraid to experiment with different recipes and ingredients to discover new and exciting flavours. You can use the air fryer to cook anything from chicken wings to vegetables, and even desserts like donuts or cakes. With a bit of creativity, you can create delicious meals that your family and friends will love.

Overall, the Ninja Dual Zone air fryer is an excellent investment for any home cook. With its versatility, ease of use, and convenient features, it's a kitchen appliance that can help you cook healthy, delicious meals with minimal fuss and mess. By following these tips and tricks, you'll be able to get the most out of your air fryer and create culinary delights that will impress even the most discerning taste buds.

FAQs

Is it safe to pull out the drawer while the food is cooking?

Absolutely! In fact, it's recommended that you do so, as you'll need to remove the drawer halfway through cooking. You can also open the drawer a few times to check on the food just before it's supposed to be done.

Does the outer part of the Ninja air fryer get hot during cooking?

Yes, it does get a little hot, but the parts that you need to touch, such as the drawer handles and control panel, are still safe to touch. However, if you're concerned about getting burned, you can use oven mitts or silicone gloves for safety.

Should I defrost frozen foods before putting them in the air fryer?

It depends on the food. Follow the instructions on the packaging, and always make sure that frozen food is cooked all the way through before serving.

Can I adjust the settings on the Ninja air fryer while it's already running?

Absolutely! You can adjust settings like temperature and cooking time while food is cooking inside the air fryer. Some recipes even suggest lowering the heat during the cooking process.

Do I need to clean the air fryer after every use?

If you line the tray with paper, foil, or a liner, you might not need to, but always check for any leftover crumbs or food before starting the air fryer again. Any leftover food can become burnt and cause damage to the trays over time.

Can an air fryer overheat?

It's possible, so make sure you give your air fryer enough space for air to circulate around it while it's in use. Most manufacturers recommend leaving about 6 inches of space all the way around the air fryer while it's cooking food.

How can I check if meat is cooked safely?

The Ninja website sells a specific thermometer for this purpose, but you can also use a regular meat thermometer to ensure that meats such as beef, pork, and lamb have an internal temperature of 65 degrees Celsius and that chicken and seafood have an internal temperature of 75 degrees Celsius.

Can I boil water in the Ninja air fryer?

Although it's technically possible, the manufacturer recommends against it for safety reasons. The fan could splash water into the air fryer's internal parts, causing it to malfunction. It's better to use a kettle instead.

Can I use toothpicks or wooden skewers in the Ninja air fryer?

Yes, you can use them. However, it's best to soak them in water for about 30 minutes before using them to prevent them from burning while inside the air fryer.

Does the Ninja air fryer emit cooking odours?

One of the best features of the Ninja air fryer is that it doesn't cause cooking odours, even when cooking fish or other strong-smelling foods. You can serve anything you like during dinner parties without worrying about unpleasant smells.

Can I layer food in the Ninja air fryer?

While it's best to cook meat in a single layer, you can cook things like chips or vegetables in layers as long as you shake them halfway through the cooking process.

Chapter 1: Breakfast Recipes

Avocado Egg Boats

Serves: 2
Prep time: 5 minutes / Cook time: 10 minutes

Ingredients:

- 2 ripe avocados, halved and pitted
- 4 medium eggs
- 2 tbsp chopped fresh chives
- Salt and black pepper, to taste

Preparation instructions:

1. Preheat the Ninja Dual Zone Air Fryer to 160°C on zone 1 for 5 minutes.
2. Use a spoon to scoop out a little bit of the avocado flesh to make room for the egg.
3. Crack an egg into each avocado half, making sure the yolk stays intact.
4. Season the eggs with salt and black pepper.
5. Sprinkle chopped chives on top of each egg.
6. Place the avocado halves on the crisper plate in zone 1 and air fry at 160°C for 10 minutes or until the egg whites are set.
7. Once cooked, remove from the air fryer and serve immediately.

Baked Oatmeal Bites

Makes: 12-14 bites
Prep time: 10 minutes / Cook time: 15 minutes

Ingredients:

- 180g rolled oats
- 120ml unsweetened applesauce
- 60ml maple syrup
- 1 egg, beaten
- 1/2 tsp baking powder
- 1/2 tsp ground cinnamon
- 1/4 tsp salt
- 120ml milk of choice
- 30g raisins (optional)

Preparation instructions:

1. Preheat the Ninja Dual Zone Air Fryer to 180°C on Air Fry mode.
2. In a mixing bowl, combine the rolled oats, baking powder, cinnamon, and salt.
3. Add the unsweetened applesauce, maple syrup, beaten egg, and milk to the bowl, and stir to combine.
4. If using, fold in the raisins.
5. Using a cookie scoop or spoon, scoop the oat mixture into silicone muffin cups, filling each cup about 3/4 full.
6. Place the muffin cups into the crisper plate of the Air Fryer and bake for 15 minutes, or until the bites are firm and lightly golden.
7. Remove from the Air Fryer and allow to cool for a few minutes before serving.

Broiled Grapefruit

Serves: 2
Prep time: 5 minutes / Cook time: 5 minutes

Ingredients:

- 1 large grapefruit
- 2 tsp brown sugar
- 1/2 tsp ground cinnamon

Preparation instructions:

1. Cut the grapefruit in half and use a sharp knife to loosen the segments.
2. Sprinkle the brown sugar and cinnamon evenly over the top of each grapefruit half.
3. Place the grapefruit halves on the crisper plate.
4. Select zone 1 and pair it with "BROIL" at 200°C for 5 minutes.
5. Select "START/STOP" to begin cooking.

Dehydrated Fruit and Nut Granola

Serves: 6

Prep time: 10 minutes / Cook time: 3-4 hours (dehydrating time)

Ingredients:

- 200g rolled oats
- 50g shredded coconut
- 50g chopped almonds
- 50g chopped walnuts
- 50g chopped dried apricots
- 50g dried cranberries
- 1/4 tsp ground cinnamon
- 60ml maple syrup
- 60ml vegetable oil

Preparation instructions:

1. In a large mixing bowl, combine the rolled oats, shredded coconut, chopped almonds, chopped walnuts, chopped dried apricots, dried cranberries, and ground cinnamon.
2. In a separate small mixing bowl, whisk together the maple syrup and vegetable oil until well combined.
3. Pour the maple syrup mixture over the dry ingredients and stir until everything is evenly coated.
4. Divide the mixture into two equal portions and place each portion on its own crisper plate.
5. Select zone 1 and pair it with "DEHYDRATE" at 60°C for 3-4 hours, or until the granola is completely dry and crispy.
6. Once done, remove from the air fryer and allow to cool before transferring to an airtight container for storage.

Dehydrated Yoghurt Drops

Makes: 20 drops

Prep time: 5 minutes / Dehydrating time: 6 hours

Ingredients:

- 100g plain Greek yoghurt
- 1 tsp honey
- 10g mixed berries (blueberries, raspberries, strawberries), chopped
- 10g granola

Preparation instructions:

1. In a small bowl, mix together the Greek yoghurt and honey until fully combined.
2. Using a piping bag or a small spoon, pipe or drop small dollops of the yoghurt mixture onto a silicone mat or a lined dehydrator tray.
3. Sprinkle each dollop with chopped mixed berries and granola.
4. Place the tray in the dehydrator and select zone 1, pairing it with the "DEHYDRATE" function at 55°C for 6 hours.
5. Once the drops are fully dehydrated, remove them from the dehydrator and store in an airtight container at room temperature.

Breakfast Bruschetta

Serves: 2

Prep time: 10 minutes / Cook time: 10 minutes

Ingredients:

- 4 slices of sourdough bread, 1cm thick
- 2 cloves of garlic, peeled and halved
- 2 medium-sized vine tomatoes, chopped
- 1 tbsp extra-virgin olive oil
- 1 tsp balsamic vinegar
- 1 tbsp fresh basil leaves, finely chopped
- 2 large eggs
- Salt and black pepper, to taste

Preparation instructions:

1. Preheat the Ninja Dual Zone Air Fryer to 180°C using the "Bake" function.
2. Cut the sourdough bread into 1cm thick slices and place them on the crisper plate of Zone 1. Air fry for 3 minutes or until slightly toasted.

3. Rub each slice of bread with the cut side of the garlic cloves.
4. In a bowl, combine the chopped tomatoes, extra-virgin olive oil, balsamic vinegar, and basil leaves. Season with salt and black pepper.
5. Spoon the tomato mixture over the toasted bread slices.
6. Crack one egg into a small bowl and carefully pour it over one of the prepared bruschetta.
7. Repeat with the second egg and bruschetta.
8. Air fry the bruschettas with the eggs in Zone 2 at 180°C using the "Bake" function for 5-7 minutes or until the eggs are cooked to your desired level.
9. Remove the bruschetta from the air fryer and serve immediately. Enjoy!

Baked Breakfast Quiche

Serves: 6

Prep time: 20 minutes / Cook time: 25 minutes

Ingredients:
- 1 tbsp olive oil
- 1 onion, diced
- 1 red bell pepper, diced
- 100g spinach leaves, washed and chopped
- 6 large eggs
- 100ml whole milk
- 50g cheddar cheese, grated
- Salt and pepper, to taste

Preparation instructions:
1. Preheat the Ninja Dual Zone Air Fryer to 180°C on zone 1 using the "BAKE" function.
2. In a frying pan, heat the olive oil and sauté the onion and red bell pepper until softened. Add the chopped spinach leaves and cook until wilted. Remove from heat and let cool.
3. In a mixing bowl, beat the eggs and whisk in the milk. Add the cooled vegetables and grated cheese. Season with salt and pepper.
4. Pour the mixture into a greased baking dish and place it on the crisper plate on zone 1.
5. Bake the quiche for 25 minutes or until set and golden brown.

Granola Bars

Makes: 8 bars

Prep time: 10 minutes / Cook time: 15 minutes

Ingredients:
- 100g rolled oats
- 50g almonds, chopped
- 50g pumpkin seeds
- 50g dried cranberries
- 50g honey
- 50g coconut oil
- 1 tsp vanilla extract

Preparation instructions:
1. Preheat the Ninja Dual Zone Air Fryer to 160°C on zone 2 using the "DEHYDRATE" function.
2. In a mixing bowl, combine the rolled oats, chopped almonds, pumpkin seeds, and dried cranberries.
3. In a small saucepan, heat the honey and coconut oil until melted. Stir in the vanilla extract.
4. Pour the honey mixture into the dry ingredients and mix well until everything is coated.
5. Spread the mixture into a greased baking dish and place it on the crisper plate on zone 2.
6. Dehydrate the granola for 15 minutes or until crisp and golden brown.
7. Let the granola cool completely before cutting it into bars.

Breakfast Scones

Makes: 8 scones

Prep time: 15 minutes / Cook time: 12 minutes

Ingredients:
- 225g self-raising flour
- 50g caster sugar

- 50g unsalted butter, cubed
- 100ml whole milk
- 1 egg, beaten
- 1 tsp vanilla extract
- 50g raisins
- Pinch of salt

Preparation instructions:

1. Preheat the Ninja Dual Zone Air Fryer to 180°C on zone 1 using the "BAKE" function.
2. In a mixing bowl, combine the self-raising flour, caster sugar, and salt.
3. Rub in the cubed butter until the mixture resembles breadcrumbs.
4. Add the raisins and mix well.
5. In a separate bowl, whisk together the milk, beaten egg, and vanilla extract.
6. Pour the wet ingredients into the dry ingredients and mix until a dough forms.
7. On a floured surface, roll out the dough to about 2cm thickness.
8. Cut the dough into 8 scones and place them on the crisper plate on zone 1.
9. Bake the scones for 12 minutes or until risen and golden brown.

Breakfast Tacos

Serves: 2

Prep time: 15 minutes / Cook time: 4-6 minutes

Ingredients:

- 4 small flour tortillas
- 4 large eggs
- 50g cheddar cheese, grated
- 1 avocado, sliced
- 4 cherry tomatoes, halved
- Salt and pepper, to taste

Preparation instructions:

1. Preheat the Ninja Dual Zone Air Fryer to 180°C on zone 1 using the "BAKE" function.
2. Warm up the flour tortillas in the air fryer for 1-2 minutes until slightly toasted.
3. In a mixing bowl, whisk the eggs and season with salt and pepper.
4. Pour the egg mixture onto the crisper plate on zone 1 and scramble the eggs using a silicone spatula.
5. Once the eggs are cooked, divide them into 4 portions and place each portion onto a tortilla.
6. Sprinkle grated cheddar cheese on top of the eggs.
7. Place the tortillas back onto the crisper plate on zone 1 and bake for 3-4 minutes until the cheese is melted.
8. Take the tortillas out of the air fryer and top them with sliced avocado and halved cherry tomatoes.
9. Fold the tortillas in half and serve.

Breakfast Avocado Bread

Serves 2

Prep time: 5 minutes / Cook time: 5-7 minutes

Ingredients

- 2 avocado
- 4 slices of bread
- 2 egg
- Salt and pepper to taste
- Optional toppings: sliced tomatoes, bacon, cheese

Instructions :

1. Preheat the Ninja Dual Zone air fryer to 175°C.
2. Slice the avocado in half, remove the pit, and scoop the flesh into a small bowl. Mash the avocado with a fork until it's smooth.
3. Add 4 slices of bread to the bowl with the mashed avocado and use a fork to coat both sides of the bread with the avocado mixture.
4. Place the bread in the air fryer basket and cook for 5-7 minutes, or until the bread is crispy and golden brown.
5. While the bread is cooking, fry an egg in a skillet

over medium heat until it's cooked to your liking. Season with salt and pepper to taste.

6. Once the bread is done, remove it from the air fryer and place it on a plate. Top with the fried egg and any additional toppings you desire, such as sliced tomatoes, bacon, or cheese.

7. Serve hot & enjoy.

Breakfast Hash Browns

Serves 4

Prep time: 10 minutes / Cook time: 15 minutes

Ingredients

- 4 medium russet potatoes, peeled and grated
- 1 small onion, grated
- 2 tablespoons all-purpose flour
- 1 teaspoon garlic powder
- 1 teaspoon paprika
- 1/2 teaspoon salt
- 1/4 teaspoon black pepper
- 2 tablespoons vegetable oil

Instructions :

1. Preheat your ninja foodi air fryer to 200°C.

2. In a large bowl, combine the grated potatoes and grated onion. Squeeze out any excess moisture with a clean dish towel.

3. Add the flour, garlic powder, paprika, salt, and black pepper to the bowl and mix well.

4. Drizzle the vegetable oil over the mixture and stir until the potatoes are evenly coated.

5. Divide the mixture into 8 equal portions and shape them into patties.

6. Place the patties in the air fryer basket in a single layer, leaving space between them for air to circulate.

7. Cook the hash browns for 10-12 minutes, or until crispy and golden brown, flipping them halfway through cooking.

8. Remove the hash browns from the air fryer and serve hot with your favorite breakfast foods, such as eggs, bacon, or toast.

9. Serve hot & enjoy.

Apple and custard crumble rolls

Serves 6

Prep time: 15 minutes / Cook time: 10 minutes

Ingredients

- 240g apple slices pie fruit
- 45g sultanas
- 1/2 tsp ground cinnamon
- 6 frozen spring roll wrappers, thawed
- 120g bought thick vanilla custard, plus extra, to serve
- 3 McVitie's Digestives The Original biscuits, finely chopped
- 25g rolled oats
- Cinnamon sugar, to serve

Instructions :

1. Combine the apple, sultanas, and cinnamon in a medium-sized bowl.

2. Take a spring roll wrapper and place it on a clean work surface with the corner closest to you. Put one-sixth of the apple mixture just below the center of the wrapper. Brush the edges with custard, fold in the sides, and roll up the wrapper to enclose the filling. Repeat the process to make a total of 6 rolls. Brush the remaining custard over the rolls.

3. Mix the oats and biscuits together on a plate. Dip each roll into the mixture.

4. Grease the air fryer basket with cooking spray. Place the rolls in the basket and spray them with cooking oil.

5. Preheat your ninja foodi air fryer for 6-7 minutes at 200°C, or until they become crispy and golden brown. Transfer the rolls to a serving platter.

6. Sprinkle cinnamon sugar over the rolls and serve with extra custard.

7. Serve hot & enjoy.

Flapjacks with Strawberry Jam

Serves 4

Prep time: 10 minutes / Cook time: 20 minutes

Ingredients

- 300g old-fashioned rolled oats
- 150g brown sugar
- 100g butter, melted
- A pinch of sea salt
- 1/4 tsp cinnamon powder
- 200g peanut butter
- 100g strawberry jam

Instructions :

1. Begin by preheating your ninja foodi air fryer to 175°C. Now, brush two baking tins with nonstick cooking spray.
2. In your processor, mix the rolled oats, sugar, butter, spices, and 100 g of peanut butter; stir until everything is well combined.
3. Spoon the batter into the prepared baking tins. Place dots of the remaining peanut butter and jam on top of the flapjacks.
4. Place one baking tin in each drawer.
5. Select zone 1 and pair it with "BAKE" at 180°C for 20 minutes. Select "MATCH" followed by the "START/STOP" button.
6. Place your flapjacks on a cooling rack for 10 minutes before slicing and serving.
7. Serve hot & enjoy.

Simple Breakfast Muffins

Serves 4

Prep time: 15 minutes / Cook time:25 minutes

Ingredients

- 1 tablespoon of oil
- 150g broccoli, finely chopped
- 1 red pepper, finely chopped
- 2 spring onions, sliced
- 6 large eggs
- 1 tablespoon of whole milk
- 1/4 teaspoon of smoked paprika
- 50g cheddar

Instructions :

1. Heat your ninja foodi air fryer to 200°C. Celsius and prepare silicon muffin cases with a thin layer of oil or melted butter.
2. Lightly fry the broccoli, pepper and spring onions in your air fryer for 5 minutes.
3. Whisk your eggs, milk, smoked paprika and half of your cheese together.
4. Add your fried broccoli, peppers and spring onions to the mixture and add half of your cheese.
5. Pour your mixture into the muffin cases then sprinkle the remaining cheese on the top of the muffins.
6. Fry in the air fryer for around 17 minutes or until the cheese is melted and the muffins are golden brown.
7. Serve hot & enjoy.

Brown Sugar & Pecan Air Fryer Apples

Serves 4

Prep time: 10 minutes / Cook time:12 minutes

Ingredients

- 4 medium-sized apples, cored and sliced
- 2 tablespoons brown sugar
- 2 tablespoons chopped pecans
- 1 teaspoon ground cinnamon
- 1 tablespoon butter, melted

Instructions :

1. In a bowl, mix the brown sugar, chopped pecans, cinnamon, and melted butter.
2. Add the sliced apples to the bowl and stir until the apples are coated with the mixture.
3. Place the coated apples in the air fryer basket and cook at 180°C for 12 minutes.
4. Serve hot & enjoy.

French Toast Cups with Raspberries:

Serves 4

Prep time: 15 minutes / Cook time:10 minutes

Ingredients

- 8 slices of bread, crusts removed
- 4 eggs
- 1/2 cup milk
- 2 tablespoons maple syrup
- 1 teaspoon vanilla extract
- 1/2 cup raspberries
- Cooking spray

Instructions :

1. Preheat the Ninja Dual Zone air fryer to 180°C.
2. Flatten the bread slices with a rolling pin and press them into the cups of a muffin tin that has been sprayed with cooking spray.
3. In a bowl, whisk together the eggs, milk, maple syrup, and vanilla extract.
4. Pour the egg mixture into each bread cup and top with raspberries.
5. Air fry at 180°C for 10 minutes.
6. Serve hot & enjoy.

Apple Pie Egg Roll

Serves 4

Prep time: 20 minutes / Cook time: 10 minutes

Ingredients

- 4 egg roll wrappers
- 2 medium apples, peeled, cored, and diced
- 1/4 cup brown sugar
- 1 teaspoon cinnamon
- 1/4 teaspoon nutmeg
- 1 tablespoon lemon juice
- 2 tablespoons butter, melted
- Powdered sugar for dusting
- Caramel sauce (optional)

Instructions :

1. Preheat your Ninja Dual Zone air fryer to 190°C.
2. In a bowl, combine diced apples, brown sugar, cinnamon, nutmeg, and lemon juice. Mix well.
3. Lay an egg roll wrapper on a clean surface,

and place 2-3 tablespoons of apple mixture in the center of the wrapper.
4. Roll the wrapper tightly around the apple mixture, tucking in the sides as you go. Repeat with remaining egg roll wrappers and apple mixture.
5. Brush the egg rolls with melted butter.
6. Place the egg rolls in the air fryer basket, making sure they don't touch each other.
7. Air fry for 8-10 minutes, flipping once halfway through cooking time, until the egg rolls are golden brown and crispy.
8. Remove from air fryer and let cool for a few minutes.
9. Dust with powdered sugar and serve with caramel sauce, if desired.

Double Cherry Mini Egg Rolls

Serves 4

Prep time: 20 minutes / Cook time: 10 minutes

Ingredients

- 8 egg roll wrappers
- 75 g dried cherries
- 75 g fresh cherries, pitted and chopped
- 2 tablespoons sugar
- 1/4 teaspoon cinnamon
- 1/4 teaspoon almond extract
- Powdered sugar for dusting
- Vanilla ice cream (optional)

Instructions :

1. Preheat your Ninja Dual Zone air fryer to 190°C.
2. In a bowl, mix together dried cherries, fresh cherries, sugar, cinnamon, and almond extract.
3. Lay an egg roll wrapper on a clean surface, and place 1-2 tablespoons of cherry mixture in the center of the wrapper.
4. Roll the wrapper tightly around the cherry mixture, tucking in the sides as you go.
5. Repeat with remaining egg roll wrappers and

cherry mixture.

6. Place the egg rolls in the air fryer basket, making sure they don't touch each other.

7. Air fry for 8-10 minutes, flipping once halfway through cooking time, until the egg rolls are golden brown and crispy.

8. Remove from air fryer and let cool for a few minutes.Dust with powdered sugar.

9. Serve with vanilla ice cream, if desired.

Bacon Omelette

Serves 4

Prep time: 10 minutes / Cook time:12 minutes

Ingredients

- 8 whole eggs
- 100g cream cheese
- 30g bacon lardons
- 1 medium onion, peeled and chopped
- 1 medium bell pepper, deseeded and chopped
- Sea salt and ground black pepper, to taste

Instructions

1. Preheat your ninja foodi air fryer to 180°C and grease 8 muffin cases very lightly with butter.

2. In a mixing bowl, thoroughly mix all the ingredients.

3. Using a spoon, fill the prepared muffin cases with the batter. Place 4 muffin cases in each drawer.

4. For 12 minutes, set Zone 1 to "BAKE" at 180°C. Click "MATCH," then press the "START/STOP" button.

5. Serve the muffins hot and enjoy!

Tropical French toast

Serves 4

Prep time: 10 minutes / Cook time:20 minutes

Ingredients

- 1 papaya
- 2 bananas
- 60ml almond milk

- 1/2 tsp ground cinnamon
- 4 eggs, lightly whisked
- 8 sourdough bread slices
- 250g natural yoghurt
- Fresh mint leaves, to serve

Instructions

1. Commence by trimming both ends of the papaya. Employ a vegetable peeler for peeling vegetables. Slice the papaya into halves and extract the seeds. Take one-half of the papaya and chop it coarsely before placing it in a blender. Reserve the other half for later use. Combine banana, almond milk, and cinnamon in a blender and blend until thoroughly mixed.

2. Blend banana, almond milk, and cinnamon in a blender until well combined.

3. In a bowl, put the eggs. Add 125ml papaya mix. Dip bread in, let excess drip. Air fry coated bread at 200°C for 5 minutes. Use the remaining bread and egg mixture in the same way.

4. In the meantime, Mix yogurt and 125ml papaya mix. Slice remaining papaya half crosswise, finely chop other half.

5. Put French toast on plate. Add yogurt and papaya mix. Repeat with another slice of toast and more mix. Top with sliced and chopped papaya. Repeat. Garnish with mint leaves.

Crispy Bacon Breakfast Muffin

Serves 4

Prep time: 15 minutes / Cook time:11 minutes

Ingredients

- 4 toasting muffin buns
- 12 slices of bacon
- 60ml tomato ketchup
- 1cal olive spray

Instructions

1. Place crisper plates into each zone draw of the ninja foodi, then preheat the unit at

200°C for 4-5 minutes

2. Toss the bacon rashers into the zone 1 draw and the toasting muffins into zone 2
3. Select zone 1 and pair it with 'AIR FRYER' at 200°C for 11 minutes
4. Select zone 2 and pair it with 'ROAST' at 160°C for 4 minutes
5. Press 'SYNC' followed by 'START/STOP' to cook the bacon and muffins
6. At the 5 minutes mark pull out the zone 1 draw and shake the bacon rashers, then leave them in to cook for the remainder 6 minutes
7. Retrieve the food content, slice the toasting muffins horizontally to create 2 layers
8. Sandwich 3 bacon rashers and 1 tbsp of ketchup in each toasting muffin to serve

Maple Cinnamon Oatmeal Breakfast Cookies

Serves 8
Prep time: 5 minutes / Cook time: 5 minutes

Ingredients
- 225g caster sugar
- 115g unsalted butter
- 120g oats
- 1 tsp vanilla extract
- 2 large eggs
- 120g all-purpose flour
- ½ tsp sea salt
- ½ tsp baking powder
- 1 ¼ tsp cinnamon
- 120ml maple syrup
- 1cal olive fry spray

Preparation Instructions
1. Preheat the ninja foodi to 180°C for 5 minutes, then carefully line the ninja foodi zone draws with parchment paper
2. Spray the parchment paper thoroughly
3. Employing a stand mixer and a large bowl, amalgamate the butter, eggs, sugar, and vanilla to form a fluffed mixture
4. Add the salt and the baking powder, then combine it using a fork
5. Toss, mix and press in the oats and maple syrup into the mixture
6. Hand mould 8 cookies and place 4 in each ninja zone draw on top of on top of the parchment paper
7. Select the zones and pair them 'BAKE' function at 180°C for 5 minutes
8. Retrieve the cookies and enjoy

Air Fried Egg & Crispy Honey Bacon

Serves 4
Prep time: 15 minutes / Cook time: 6 minutes

Ingredients
- 4 large eggs
- ¼ tsp sea salt
- ⅛ tbsp ground black pepper
- 8 slices of bacon
- 60g honey
- 1cal olive spray

Preparation Instructions
1. Place the crisper plates in the zone 2 draw
2. Employ a suitable baking pan for the ninja duel zone and spray thoroughly with 1cal fry spray
3. Crack the eggs and carefully place them into the baking pan
4. Submerge the bacon slices in the honey
5. Place the egg pan into the zone 1 draw and honey bacon in zone 2
6. Select zone 1 and 'AIR FRY' at 180°C for 8 minutes
7. Select zone 2 and 'AIR FRY' at 180°C for 10 minutes
8. Press 'SYNC' followed by 'STOP/START' to air fry the food content
9. Half way through cooking, flip the bacon
10. Retrieve the food content and cut out the eggs to plate them up (1 per plate)
11. Place the crispy honey bacon besides the egg to serve (2 slices per plate)

Chapter 2: Main Courses

Chimichangas

Serves: 4

Prep time: 20 minutes / Cook time: 16 minutes

Ingredients:

- 4 large flour tortillas
- 300g cooked and shredded chicken
- 120g cooked rice
- 120g black beans, drained and rinsed
- 120g sweetcorn
- 1/2 red onion, finely chopped
- 2 cloves garlic, minced
- 1/2 red bell pepper, finely chopped
- 1/2 green bell pepper, finely chopped
- 1 tsp ground cumin
- 1 tsp smoked paprika
- 1/4 tsp chilli powder
- 120g shredded cheddar cheese
- 1 tbsp olive oil
- Salt and pepper, to taste
- Fresh coriander leaves, to serve

Preparation instructions:

1. Preheat the Ninja Dual Zone Air Fryer to 200°C on zone 1 using the "AIR FRY" function.
2. In a large skillet, heat the olive oil over medium-high heat. Add the red onion, garlic, and bell peppers and cook for 3-4 minutes until softened.
3. Add the shredded chicken, cooked rice, black beans, sweetcorn, cumin, smoked paprika, and chilli powder to the skillet. Season with salt and pepper to taste. Cook for another 2-3 minutes until the mixture is heated through.
4. Spoon the mixture evenly onto each flour tortilla. Sprinkle shredded cheddar cheese over the filling.

5. Roll up the tortillas, tucking in the sides to form a tight burrito shape. Secure each chimichanga with toothpicks.
6. Place the chimichangas on the crisper plate on zone 1 and air fry for 8 minutes until crispy and golden brown.
7. Serve hot, topped with fresh coriander leaves.

Chicken Cordon Bleu

Serves: 2

Prep time: 20 minutes / Cook time: 20 minutes

Ingredients:

- 2 chicken breasts
- 4 slices of cooked ham
- 4 slices of Swiss cheese
- 1 tsp Dijon mustard
- 1 tbsp fresh parsley, chopped
- 1 tsp garlic powder
- 1 tsp paprika
- 1/2 tsp salt
- 1/4 tsp black pepper
- 60g plain flour
- 1 egg, beaten
- 50g breadcrumbs
- 1 tbsp olive oil

Preparation instructions:

1. Preheat the Ninja Dual Zone Air Fryer to 200°C using the "ROAST" function.
2. Using a sharp knife, make a horizontal slit on the side of each chicken breast to create a pocket.
3. Spread 1/2 tsp of Dijon mustard inside each pocket.
4. Stuff each pocket with 2 slices of ham and 2 slices of Swiss cheese.

5. In a small bowl, mix the parsley, garlic powder, paprika, salt, and black pepper.
6. In a separate shallow dish, mix the flour with 1/2 of the spice mixture.
7. In a third shallow dish, beat the egg.
8. In a fourth shallow dish, mix the breadcrumbs with the remaining spice mixture. Coat each stuffed chicken breast in the flour mixture, then dip in the beaten egg, and finally coat in the breadcrumb mixture, making sure it is well coated.
9. Place the coated chicken breasts on the Air Fryer basket, making sure they are not touching each other.
10. Drizzle olive oil over the chicken breasts.
11. Place the basket in the Ninja Dual Zone Air Fryer and select the "ROAST" function. Set the cooking time to 20 minutes.
12. After 10 minutes, flip the chicken breasts over using a pair of tongs to ensure even cooking.
13. Once the cooking time is up, remove the chicken breasts from the Air Fryer and let them rest for a few minutes before slicing and serving.
14. Enjoy your delicious Chicken Cordon Bleu!

Korean Fried Chicken

Serves: 2-3

Prep time: 15 minutes / Cook time: 20 minutes

Ingredients:
- 1 lb chicken wings, cut into drumettes and flats
- 1 tsp salt
- 1 tsp ground black pepper
- 1 tsp garlic powder
- 1 tsp onion powder
- 1 tsp paprika
- 120g cup all-purpose flour
- 120g cornstarch
- 1 egg
- 60m water
- 1 tbsp rice vinegar
- 60ml gochujang sauce
- 1 tbsp honey
- 1 tsp sesame oil
- 1 tbsp soy sauce
- 1 tsp grated ginger
- 1 tbsp corn syrup
- 1 tsp toasted sesame seeds

Preparation instructions:
1. Preheat the Ninja Dual Zone Air Fryer on "Fry" mode at 200°C for 5 minutes.
2. In a large bowl, mix together the salt, black pepper, garlic powder, onion powder, and paprika.
3. In another bowl, whisk together the flour, cornstarch, egg, water, and 1/2 tsp of the spice mixture until smooth.
4. Coat the chicken in the flour mixture and place in the air fryer basket. Fry for 10 minutes in Zone 1, then transfer to Zone 2 and fry for another 10 minutes, until golden brown and crispy.
6. In a small saucepan, combine the rice vinegar, gochujang sauce, honey, sesame oil, soy sauce, ginger, corn syrup, and remaining spice mixture. Cook over medium heat until thickened, about 5 minutes.
7. Toss the fried chicken with the sauce and sprinkle with sesame seeds. Serve hot.

Salmon Teriyaki

Serves: 2-3

Prep time: 10 minutes / Cook time: 12 minutes

Ingredients:
- 2 salmon fillets
- 1 tbsp vegetable oil
- 1 tbsp soy sauce

- 1 tbsp sake
- 1 tbsp mirin
- 1 tbsp sugar
- 1 tbsp honey
- 1 tsp grated ginger
- 1 clove garlic, minced
- 1 tbsp cornstarch
- 1 tbsp water
- Sliced scallions and sesame seeds, for garnish

Preparation instructions:

1. Preheat the Ninja Dual Zone Air Fryer on "Roast" mode at 200°C for 5 minutes.
2. In a small saucepan, combine the soy sauce, sake, mirin, sugar, honey, ginger, and garlic. Cook over medium heat until thickened, about 5 minutes.
3. Brush the salmon fillets with oil and place in the air fryer basket. Roast for 6 minutes in Zone 1, then transfer to Zone 2 and roast for another 6 minutes.
4. In a small bowl, mix the cornstarch and water until smooth. Add to the saucepan with the sauce and cook for an additional minute, stirring constantly until the sauce thickens.
5. Once the salmon is done, remove it from the air fryer basket and brush the teriyaki sauce over it.
6. Garnish with sliced scallions and sesame seeds.
7. Serve the salmon teriyaki hot with your choice of sides, such as steamed rice and sautéed vegetables. Enjoy!

Tandoori Chicken Thighs

Serves: 4

Prep time: 15 minutes / Marinate time: 4 hours / Cook time: 20 minutes

Ingredients:

- 1 kg bone-in chicken thighs
- 2 tbsp tandoori masala powder
- 1 tsp ground cumin
- 1 tsp ground coriander
- 1 tsp paprika
- 1/2 tsp turmeric
- 1/2 tsp salt
- 2 tbsp lemon juice
- 4 garlic cloves, minced
- 1-inch piece ginger, grated
- 120g plain yoghurt
- 2 tbsp vegetable oil
- Lemon wedges and fresh cilantro leaves, for serving

Preparation instructions:

1. In a large bowl, mix together the tandoori masala powder, cumin, coriander, paprika, turmeric, and salt.
2. Add the lemon juice, minced garlic, grated ginger, yoghurt, and vegetable oil to the bowl and mix until well combined.
3. Add the chicken thighs to the bowl and coat them with the marinade. Cover the bowl with cling film and refrigerate for at least 4 hours or overnight.
4. When ready to cook, preheat zone 1 of the Ninja Dual Zone Air Fryer to 200°C on the Roast function for 5 minutes.
5. Remove the chicken thighs from the marinade and shake off any excess. Place the chicken on the crisper plate in zone 1 of the air fryer and roast for 10 minutes.
6. While the chicken is cooking, preheat zone 2 of the Ninja Dual Zone Air Fryer to 200°C on the Roast function for 5 minutes.
7. After 10 minutes, move the crisper plate to zone 2 of the air fryer and continue roasting for an additional 10 minutes or until the chicken is cooked through and the skin is crispy.

8. Serve the chicken with lemon wedges and fresh cilantro leaves on the side.

9. Note: If you don't have tandoori masala powder, you can make your own by mixing together 1 tsp ground cumin, 1 tsp ground coriander, 1 tsp paprika, 1/2 tsp turmeric, and 1/2 tsp cayenne pepper.

Sesame-Ginger Beef Skewers

Serves: 4

Prep time: 20 minutes / Cook time: 15 minutes

Ingredients:

- 500g beef sirloin, cut into 2.5cm cubes
- 2 tablespoons sesame oil
- 2 tablespoons soy sauce
- 1 tablespoon rice vinegar
- 2 teaspoons honey
- 1 teaspoon grated fresh ginger
- 1 teaspoon minced garlic
- 1/4 teaspoon red pepper flakes
- 1/4 teaspoon salt
- 1/4 teaspoon black pepper
- 2 bell peppers, cut into 2.5cm pieces
- 1 red onion, cut into 2.5cm pieces
- 8 skewers

Preparation instructions:

1. Soak the skewers in water for at least 20 minutes before use.

2. Preheat zone 1 of your Ninja Dual Zone Air Fryer on broil setting for 5 minutes.

3. In a mixing bowl, combine the sesame oil, soy sauce, rice vinegar, honey, ginger, garlic, red pepper flakes, salt, and black pepper. Whisk until well combined.

4. Add the beef cubes to the marinade and toss to coat evenly. Let it marinate for at least 15 minutes, or up to 2 hours in the fridge.

5. Thread the beef cubes, bell peppers, and red onion onto the skewers, alternating them as

desired.

6. Place the skewers on the crisper plate in zone 1 of the air fryer and broil for 5-7 minutes on each side, or until the beef is cooked to your liking.

7. Preheat zone 2 of your air fryer on roast setting for 5 minutes.

8. Place the skewers in zone 2 of the air fryer and roast at 200°C for 5-8 minutes, or until the vegetables are tender and slightly charred.

9. Remove the skewers from the air fryer and let them rest for 5 minutes before serving.

10. Enjoy your delicious Sesame-Ginger Beef Skewers!

Baked Cajun Shrimp and Sausage Foil Packets

Serves: 2

Prep time: 15 minutes / Cook time: 20 minutes

Ingredients:

- 200g raw shrimp, peeled and deveined
- 2 spicy sausages, sliced
- 1 red bell pepper, chopped
- 1 green bell pepper, chopped
- 1 small onion, chopped
- 2 cloves garlic, minced
- 1 tsp Cajun seasoning
- 1 tsp smoked paprika
- 1/4 tsp cayenne pepper
- 1/4 tsp dried thyme
- 2 tbsp olive oil
- Salt and black pepper, to taste
- Fresh parsley, chopped for garnish

Preparation instructions:

1. Preheat the Ninja Dual Zone Air Fryer to 200°C using the "ROAST" function.

2. Cut 2 sheets of aluminium foil (about 30cm

long) and place them on a flat surface.

3. In a medium bowl, combine the shrimp, sausage, bell peppers, onion, garlic, Cajun seasoning, smoked paprika, cayenne pepper, thyme, olive oil, salt and pepper. Toss to coat.

4. Divide the mixture equally between the foil sheets and fold them tightly to make packets.

5. Place the packets on the crisper plate in zone 1 and select the "ROAST" function for 20 minutes.

6. When the cooking is finished, carefully remove the packets from the Ninja Dual Zone Air Fryer.

7. Open the packets and sprinkle fresh parsley on top. Serve hot.

8. Enjoy your Baked Cajun Shrimp and Sausage Foil Packets cooked to perfection in the Ninja Dual Zone Air Fryer!

Roasted Turkey Breast with Cranberry Glaze

Serves: 4-6

Prep time: 10 minutes / Cook time: 60 minutes

Ingredients:

- 1 (1kg) boneless turkey breast
- 2 tbsp olive oil
- 1 tsp dried thyme
- 1 tsp dried rosemary
- 1 tsp garlic powder
- 1 tsp onion powder
- 1 tsp paprika
- Salt and black pepper, to taste
- 100g cranberry sauce
- 2 tbsp honey
- 2 tbsp soy sauce
- 2 tbsp apple cider vinegar
- 1 tbsp cornstarch
- 2 tbsp cold water

Preparation instructions:

1. Preheat the Ninja Dual Zone Air Fryer to 180°C in zone 1 for 5 minutes.

2. In a small bowl, mix together olive oil, thyme, rosemary, garlic powder, onion powder, paprika, salt, and black pepper. Rub the mixture all over the turkey breast.

3. Place the turkey breast onto the crisper plate in zone 1 of the air fryer. Roast for 45 minutes.

4. Meanwhile, in a small saucepan, whisk together cranberry sauce, honey, soy sauce, and apple cider vinegar. Bring to a boil and simmer for 5 minutes until thickened.

5. In another small bowl, whisk together cornstarch and cold water until smooth. Add the cornstarch mixture to the cranberry glaze and whisk until thickened. Remove from heat.

6. After 45 minutes of cooking the turkey, remove the crisper plate from zone 1 of the air fryer and brush the turkey breast with the cranberry glaze. Return to the air fryer and roast for another 10-15 minutes or until the turkey reaches an internal temperature of 75°C.

7. Once done, remove the turkey from the air fryer and let it rest for 5-10 minutes before slicing and serving with the remaining cranberry glaze on the side.

8. Enjoy your delicious roasted turkey breast with cranberry glaze, made easily and quickly using the Ninja Dual Zone Air Fryer!

Blackened Mahi-Mahi Tacos

Serves: 4

Prep time: 15 minutes / Cook time: 10 minutes

Ingredients:
For the Mahi-Mahi:
- 4 (150g each) Mahi-Mahi fillets

- 2 tbsp olive oil
- 2 tsp paprika
- 1 tsp garlic powder
- 1 tsp onion powder
- 1 tsp dried oregano
- 1 tsp ground cumin
- 1/2 tsp sea salt
- 1/4 tsp cayenne pepper

For the Tacos:
- 8 small corn tortillas
- 1 avocado, diced
- 1/4 red onion, thinly sliced
- 1 jalapeño, seeded and diced
- 1 lime, cut into wedges
- 60g fresh cilantro, chopped
- Sea salt and ground black pepper, to taste

Preparation instructions:

1. Preheat your Ninja Dual Zone Air Fryer to 200°C on BROIL function.
2. In a small bowl, mix together paprika, garlic powder, onion powder, oregano, cumin, sea salt, and cayenne pepper to make the seasoning for the Mahi-Mahi.
3. Rub the seasoning over both sides of the Mahi-Mahi fillets and drizzle them with olive oil.
4. Place the fillets on the crisper plate in Zone 1 and broil for 10 minutes or until they are cooked through and blackened.
5. While the fish is cooking, heat the tortillas in Zone 2 using the BAKE function at 180°C for 2 minutes.
6. To assemble the tacos, place the cooked Mahi-Mahi on the warm tortillas and top with diced avocado, thinly sliced red onion, diced jalapeño, and chopped cilantro.
7. Squeeze fresh lime juice over the tacos and season with salt and black pepper, to taste.
8. Serve immediately and enjoy your delicious Blackened Mahi-Mahi Tacos!

Panko-Crusted Salmon with Honey-Mustard Glaze

Serves: 2

Prep time: 10 minutes / Cook time: 20 minutes

Ingredients:
- 2 (150g each) skinless salmon fillets
- 50g panko breadcrumbs
- 1 tbsp olive oil
- Sea salt and ground black pepper, to taste
- 1 tbsp dijon mustard
- 1 tbsp honey
- 1 tsp fresh lemon juice
- 1 garlic clove, minced
- 1 tsp dried thyme leaves

Preparation instructions:

1. Preheat the Ninja Dual Zone Air Fryer to 200°C on zone 1 for 5 minutes.
2. Season the salmon fillets with salt and pepper.
3. In a shallow dish, mix the panko breadcrumbs with olive oil, minced garlic, dried thyme, salt and pepper.
4. Coat the salmon fillets in the panko mixture, pressing lightly to adhere.
5. Place the salmon fillets on the crisper plate and spray with a little oil.
6. In a small bowl, whisk together the dijon mustard, honey, and lemon juice.
7. Select zone 1 and pair it with "AIR FRY" at 200°C for 10 minutes.
8. After 10 minutes, brush the honey-mustard glaze on top of the salmon fillets and return them to the Ninja Dual Zone Air Fryer on zone 1.
9. Select zone 2 and pair it with "AIR FRY" at 200°C for an additional 10 minutes or until the salmon is cooked through and golden brown.
10. Serve hot with your favourite side dishes.

11. Enjoy your delicious and easy Panko-Crusted Salmon with Honey-Mustard Glaze made in the Ninja Dual Zone Air Fryer!

Vegetable and Chickpea Fritters

Serves: 4

Prep time: 20 minutes / Cook time: 20 minutes

Ingredients:

- 1 can (400g) chickpeas, drained and rinsed
- 1 medium carrot, grated
- 1 medium zucchini, grated
- 1/2 red onion, finely chopped
- 2 cloves garlic, minced
- 60g chopped fresh parsley
- 60g chopped fresh cilantro
- 1 tsp ground cumin
- 1/2 tsp ground coriander
- 1/4 tsp cayenne pepper
- 120g plain flour
- 1 tsp baking powder
- 1/2 tsp salt
- 1 large egg, beaten
- 60ml milk
- 2 tbsp olive oil

Preparation instructions:

1. In a large bowl, mash the chickpeas with a fork or potato masher until they are mostly broken up, but still have some texture.
2. Add the grated carrot and zucchini, chopped onion, minced garlic, chopped parsley and cilantro, ground cumin, ground coriander, and cayenne pepper. Stir to combine.
3. In a separate bowl, whisk together the flour, baking powder, and salt.
4. Add the dry ingredients to the chickpea mixture, and stir to combine.
5. In a small bowl, whisk together the egg and milk. Add to the chickpea mixture, and stir until well combined.
6. Preheat the Ninja Dual Zone Air Fryer to 200°C using the "AIR FRY" function.
7. Using a spoon or cookie scoop, form the chickpea mixture into 8 fritters.
8. Brush the fritters with olive oil, and place them in the air fryer basket in a single layer.
9. Select zone 1 and pair it with "AIR FRY" at 200°C for 10 minutes. Select zone 2 and pair it with "AIR FRY" at 200°C for another 10 minutes. Flip the fritters halfway through the cooking time.
10. Serve the fritters hot, with a dollop of yoghurt sauce or hummus, if desired. Enjoy!

Tofu Banh Mi Sandwiches

Serves: 4

Prep time: 15 minutes / Cook time: 10 minutes

Ingredients:

- 8 oz. firm tofu, drained and pressed
- 4 small baguettes
- 120g of shredded carrots
- 120g of sliced cucumber
- 1 jalapeno, thinly sliced
- 60g of cilantro leaves
- 60g of mayonnaise
- 2 tbsp of soy sauce
- 1 tbsp of honey
- 1 garlic clove, minced
- 1 tsp of grated ginger
- Salt and pepper to taste

Preparation instructions:

1. Preheat your Ninja Dual Zone Air Fryer to 200°C on broil setting.
2. Cut the tofu into 1/2 inch slices.
3. In a small bowl, whisk together the soy sauce, honey, garlic, and ginger to make a marinade.

4. Marinate the tofu in the mixture for 10-15 minutes.
5. Arrange the tofu slices on the crisper plate in the air fryer and broil for 8-10 minutes, flipping halfway through.
6. While the tofu is cooking, slice the baguettes and spread mayonnaise on one side of each.
7. Layer shredded carrots, sliced cucumber, jalapeno, and cilantro on top of the mayonnaise.
8. When the tofu is finished, add two slices of tofu to each baguette.
9. Season with salt and pepper to taste.
10. Serve and enjoy your delicious Tofu Banh Mi Sandwiches!
11. Note: You can use other condiments like sriracha or pickled vegetables to personalise your sandwich.

Vegan Falafel

Serves: 4

Prep time: 15 minutes / Cook time: 15 minutes

Ingredients:

- 2 cans of chickpeas, drained and rinsed
- 1 small onion, roughly chopped
- 3 cloves of garlic, minced
- 1 teaspoon ground cumin
- 1 teaspoon ground coriander
- 1/2 teaspoon paprika
- 1/2 teaspoon salt
- 1/4 teaspoon black pepper
- 2 tablespoons all-purpose flour
- 2 tablespoons fresh parsley, finely chopped
- 1 tablespoon lemon juice
- 2 tablespoons olive oil

Preparation instructions:

1. Add the chickpeas, onion, garlic, cumin, coriander, paprika, salt, and pepper to a food processor. Pulse until coarsely ground.

2. Add the flour, parsley, and lemon juice to the mixture and pulse again until everything is well combined.
3. Using your hands, shape the mixture into small balls and then flatten them slightly to make discs.
4. Preheat the Ninja Dual Zone Air Fryer on zone 1 to 190°C for 5 minutes.
5. Brush the falafels with olive oil and place them in zone 1 of the air fryer.
6. Air fry the falafels for 12 minutes or until golden brown, turning them over halfway through the cooking time.
7. Serve hot with pita bread, hummus, and a salad.

Butternut Squash and Black Bean Tacos

Serves: 4

Prep time: 15 minutes / Cook time: 25 minutes

Ingredients:

- 1 small butternut squash, peeled, seeded, and cut into small cubes
- 1 red onion, chopped
- 1 red bell pepper, seeded and chopped
- 2 garlic cloves, minced
- 1 tablespoon chilli powder
- 1 teaspoon ground cumin
- 1/2 teaspoon salt
- 1 can of black beans, drained and rinsed
- 1 lime, juiced
- 8 small corn tortillas
- 1 avocado, diced
- Fresh cilantro, chopped
- Hot sauce, to taste

Preparation instructions:

1. Preheat the Ninja Dual Zone Air Fryer on zone 1 to 200°C for 5 minutes.

2. In a large bowl, mix together the butternut squash, onion, red bell pepper, garlic, chilli powder, cumin, and salt until everything is well coated.
3. Spread the vegetable mixture out on zone 1 of the air fryer and roast for 20 minutes, stirring occasionally.
4. Add the black beans to the vegetable mixture and stir to combine. Air fry for an additional 5 minutes until the beans are warmed through.
5. Warm the tortillas in zone 2 of the air fryer for 1-2 minutes.
6. Assemble the tacos by placing a spoonful of the vegetable and bean mixture in each tortilla. Top with diced avocado, cilantro, a squeeze of lime, and hot sauce, if desired.

Vegan Meatballs made with Lentils and Vegetables

Serves: 4

Prep time: 20 minutes / Cook time: 20 minutes

Ingredients:
- For the Meatballs:
- 1 can (400g) lentils, drained and rinsed
- 1 onion, chopped
- 2 garlic cloves, minced
- 1 large carrot, peeled and grated
- 1 large courgette, grated
- 1 tsp smoked paprika
- 1 tsp dried oregano
- 1 tbsp tomato puree
- 60g breadcrumbs
- Salt and pepper to taste
- 2 tbsp olive oil
- For the Sauce:
- 1 can (400g) chopped tomatoes
- 2 garlic cloves, minced
- 1 tsp smoked paprika

- Salt and pepper to taste
- Fresh basil leaves for garnish

Preparation instructions:
1. Preheat your Ninja Dual Zone Air Fryer to 180°C on Broil mode.
2. In a food processor, combine the lentils, onion, garlic, carrot, and courgette. Pulse until roughly chopped but not pureed.
3. Add the paprika, oregano, tomato puree, breadcrumbs, salt, and pepper to the mixture. Pulse until well combined.
4. Shape the mixture into golf ball-sized meatballs.
5. Brush the meatballs with olive oil and arrange them on the crisper plate.
6. Cook for 15 minutes or until golden brown, turning once halfway through.
7. In the meantime, prepare the sauce. In a saucepan, combine the chopped tomatoes, garlic, paprika, salt, and pepper. Cook on medium heat for 5-10 minutes until the sauce thickens.
8. Serve the meatballs with the sauce and garnish with fresh basil leaves.

Stuffed Peppers with Rice, Beans and Vegetables

Serves: 4

Prep time: 20 minutes / Cook time: 30 minutes

Ingredients:
- 4 bell peppers, halved and seeded
- 200g brown rice, cooked
- 1 can (400g) black beans, drained and rinsed
- 1 onion, chopped
- 2 garlic cloves, minced
- 1 large carrot, peeled and grated
- 1 large courgette, grated
- 1 tsp ground cumin

- 1 tsp smoked paprika
- 1 tbsp tomato puree
- Salt and pepper to taste
- 2 tbsp olive oil

Preparation instructions:

1. Preheat your Ninja Dual Zone Air Fryer to 200°C on Roast mode.
2. In a pan, sauté the onion and garlic in olive oil until softened.
3. Add the grated carrot and courgette to the pan and sauté until soft.
4. Add the cooked rice, black beans, cumin, paprika, tomato puree, salt, and pepper to the pan. Stir until well combined.
5. Fill each halved bell pepper with the rice and bean mixture.
6. Brush the peppers with olive oil and arrange them on the crisper plate.
7. Cook for 25-30 minutes or until the peppers are tender and slightly charred.
8. Serve hot and enjoy!

Dehydrated Air Fryer Beef Jerky

Serves: 4

Prep time: 20 minutes / Cook time: 3 hours

Ingredients:

- 1 pound lean beef, cut into thin strips
- 60ml Worcestershire sauce
- 60ml soy sauce
- 1/2 teaspoon onion powder
- 1/2 teaspoon garlic powder
- 1/2 teaspoon black pepper
- 1/4 teaspoon cayenne pepper (optional)

Preparation instructions:

1. In a bowl, mix together the Worcestershire sauce, soy sauce, onion powder, garlic powder, black pepper, and cayenne pepper

(if using).
2. Add the beef strips to the marinade, making sure each strip is well coated. Cover and refrigerate for at least 2 hours, or overnight.
3. Preheat the Ninja Dual Zone Air Fryer to 70°C using the dehydrate function.
4. Remove the beef strips from the marinade and pat them dry with paper towels. Arrange the strips on the dehydrating rack in a single layer, making sure they don't overlap.
5. Dehydrate the beef strips for 3 hours, or until they are dry and chewy. Check on them every hour and rotate the racks if necessary.
6. Once done, let the beef jerky cool down and store in an airtight container at room temperature.

Fried Black Pudding

Serves: 2

Prep time: 10 minutes / Cook time: 20 minutes

Ingredients:

- 200g black pudding, sliced
- 1 egg, beaten
- 100g breadcrumbs
- 50g plain flour
- Salt and pepper, to taste
- 2 tablespoons vegetable oil

Preparation instructions:

1. Set up a breading station by placing the beaten egg in a shallow dish, the plain flour in another shallow dish, and the breadcrumbs in a third shallow dish. Season the breadcrumbs with salt and pepper.
2. Coat each slice of black pudding with flour, then dip it in the egg, and finally coat it with the breadcrumbs. Press the breadcrumbs onto the black pudding to make sure they stick.
3. Preheat the Ninja Dual Zone Air Fryer to

200°C using the air fry function.

4. Spray the black pudding slices with vegetable oil on both sides.

5. Place the black pudding slices on the crisper plate and air fry for 10 minutes on zone 1, then flip them over and air fry for another 10 minutes on zone 2.

6. Once done, remove the black pudding from the air fryer and let them cool on a paper towel to absorb any excess oil. Serve hot with your favourite dipping sauce.

Baked Honey Mustard Salmon Fillets in the Air Fryer

Serves: 2

Prep time: 5 minutes / Cook time: 12 minutes

Ingredients:

- 2 (170g each) salmon fillets
- 2 tbsp honey
- 2 tbsp dijon mustard
- 1 tsp olive oil
- 1/2 tsp garlic powder
- Salt and pepper, to taste

Preparation instructions:

1. Preheat the Ninja Dual Zone Air Fryer to 200°C.

2. In a small bowl, mix together honey, dijon mustard, olive oil, garlic powder, salt, and pepper.

3. Place salmon fillets in the air fryer basket and brush them with the honey mustard mixture.

4. Place the basket in Zone 1 of the air fryer and select "AIR FRY" for 12 minutes.

5. Once the time is up, remove the basket from the air fryer and let it rest for a few minutes before serving.

Broiled Lobster Tails with Lemon Butter Sauce

Serves: 2

Prep time: 10 minutes / Cook time: 8 minutes

Ingredients:

- 2 lobster tails
- 2 tbsp butter
- 1 tbsp lemon juice
- 1/2 tsp garlic powder
- Salt and pepper, to taste

Preparation instructions:

1. Preheat the Ninja Dual Zone Air Fryer to 200°C on broil mode.

2. Cut the lobster tails in half lengthwise with kitchen shears.

3. In a small bowl, melt butter and mix it with lemon juice, garlic powder, salt, and pepper.

4. Brush the lobster tails with the butter mixture.

5. Place the lobster tails in Zone 2 of the air fryer and select "BROIL" for 8 minutes.

6. Once the lobster tails are cooked, remove them from the air fryer and serve with the remaining lemon butter sauce.

Seafood Paella

Serves: 4

Prep time: 15 minutes / Cook time: 30 minutes

Ingredients:
- 400g paella rice
- 800ml fish or chicken stock
- 2 tbsp olive oil
- 1 onion, finely chopped
- 3 garlic cloves, minced
- 1 red bell pepper, chopped
- 1 tsp smoked paprika
- 400g can chopped tomatoes
- 250g raw king prawns, shelled and deveined
- 250g mussels, scrubbed and debearded
- 150g squid, sliced into rings
- Salt and black pepper, to taste
- Lemon wedges, for serving

Preparation instructions:
1. In the Ninja Dual Zone Air Fryer, select zone 1 and choose the "SAUTÉ" function. Heat the olive oil and sauté the onion and garlic for 2-3 minutes until softened.
2. Add the chopped red bell pepper and continue sautéing for another 2-3 minutes until slightly softened.
3. Add the smoked paprika, canned chopped tomatoes, and paella rice. Stir until the rice is coated with the sauce.
4. Pour in the fish or chicken stock and stir until well combined.
5. Select zone 1 and choose the "ROAST" function at 200°C for 10 minutes. After 10 minutes, add the prawns, mussels, and squid, arranging them on top of the rice mixture.
6. Return the crisper plate to zone 1 and choose the "ROAST" function at 200°C for an additional 10 minutes or until the seafood is cooked through and the rice is tender and fluffy.
7. Season with salt and black pepper, to taste. Serve hot with lemon wedges.

Shrimp and Scallop Skewers with Chimichurri Sauce

Serves: 4

Prep time: 20 minutes / Cook time: 10 minutes

Ingredients:
- 16 large shrimp, peeled and deveined
- 16 large sea scallops
- 1 red onion, cut into large chunks
- 1 red bell pepper, cut into large chunks
- 1 yellow bell pepper, cut into large chunks
- 1 green bell pepper, cut into large chunks
- 2 tbsp olive oil
- Salt and black pepper, to taste
- Lemon wedges, for serving

Chimichurri Sauce:
- 240g fresh parsley leaves, chopped
- 120g fresh cilantro leaves, chopped
- 4 garlic cloves, minced
- 60ml red wine vinegar
- 120ml cup olive oil
- Salt and black pepper, to taste

Preparation instructions:
1. In a small bowl, combine all the ingredients for the chimichurri sauce. Mix well and set aside.
2. In the Ninja Dual Zone Air Fryer, select zone 1 and choose the "AIR FRY" function at 200°C for 5 minutes to preheat.
3. Thread the shrimp, scallops, red onion, and bell peppers onto skewers, alternating between the ingredients.
4. Drizzle the skewers with olive oil and season with salt and black pepper.
5. Place the skewers onto the crisper plate

and select zone 1. Choose the "AIR FRY" function at 200°C for 5 minutes. After 5 minutes, turn the skewers over and continue cooking for an additional 5 minutes.

6. Remove the skewers from the air fryer and serve hot with the chimichurri sauce and lemon wedges on the side.

Sesame-Crusted Ahi Tuna

Serves: 2

Prep time: 10 minutes / Cook time: 8 minutes

Ingredients:

- 2 (150g each) ahi tuna steaks
- 2 tbsp sesame seeds
- 1/4 tsp salt
- 1/4 tsp black pepper
- 1/4 tsp garlic powder
- 1/4 tsp onion powder
- 1/4 tsp paprika
- 1/4 tsp cayenne pepper
- 1 tbsp olive oil

Preparation instructions:

1. Preheat the Ninja Dual Zone Air Fryer to 200°C on the "BROIL" function.
2. In a shallow dish, mix together sesame seeds, salt, black pepper, garlic powder, onion powder, paprika, and cayenne pepper.
3. Brush the tuna steaks with olive oil, and then coat them evenly with the sesame seed mixture.
4. Place the coated tuna steaks on the crisper plate in Zone 1 of the air fryer.
5. Broil the tuna steaks for 4 minutes, then flip them over and broil for an additional 4 minutes.
6. Serve the sesame-crusted ahi tuna steaks with your favourite side dish.

Spicy Cajun Catfish

Serves: 2

Prep time: 10 minutes / Cook time: 12 minutes

Ingredients:

- 2 (170g each) catfish fillets
- 60g all-purpose flour
- 60g yellow cornmeal
- 1/2 tsp paprika
- 1/2 tsp garlic powder
- 1/2 tsp onion powder
- 1/2 tsp dried oregano
- 1/2 tsp dried thyme
- 1/2 tsp cayenne pepper
- 1/4 tsp salt
- 1/4 tsp black pepper
- 1 small egg, beaten
- 1 tbsp olive oil

Preparation instructions:

1. Pat the catfish fillets dry with a paper towel.
2. In a shallow dish, mix together flour, cornmeal, paprika, garlic powder, onion powder, oregano, thyme, cayenne pepper, salt, and black pepper.
3. Dip each catfish fillet into the beaten egg, and then coat both sides with the flour mixture.
4. Brush the crisper plate with olive oil, and then place the coated catfish fillets on it in Zone 1 of the air fryer.
5. Roast the catfish fillets on "ROAST" function at 200°C for 6 minutes.
6. Flip the catfish fillets over and continue roasting for an additional 6 minutes.
7. Serve the spicy cajun catfish fillets with your favourite side dish.

Beer-Battered Fish Tacos

Serves: 4

Prep time: 15 minutes / Cook time: 20 minutes

Ingredients:

- 450g white fish fillets (cod or haddock)
- 250ml beer
- 1 large egg
- 200g plain flour
- 2 tsp baking powder

- 1 tsp smoked paprika
- 1/2 tsp cumin
- 1/2 tsp garlic powder
- 1/2 tsp onion powder
- 1/2 tsp sea salt
- 1/4 tsp black pepper
- 8 small flour tortillas
- 1 avocado, sliced
- 1/4 red cabbage, shredded
- 1 lime, cut into wedges
- 1 tbsp olive oil

Preparation instructions:

1. Pat the fish fillets dry with a paper towel and cut them into small, taco-sized pieces.
2. In a bowl, whisk together the beer and egg until combined.
3. In a separate bowl, mix together the flour, baking powder, smoked paprika, cumin, garlic powder, onion powder, sea salt, and black pepper.
4. Pour the beer mixture into the flour mixture and whisk until smooth.
5. Dip each piece of fish into the batter, shaking off any excess.
6. Preheat the Ninja Dual Zone Air Fryer to 200°C using the "AIR FRY" function.
7. Place the battered fish in the crisper plate and spray with olive oil.
8. Select zone 1 and set the time to 10 minutes. Select "AIR FRY" at 200°C and press "START/STOP" to begin cooking.
9. While the fish cooks, warm the tortillas in the microwave or on a griddle.
10. When the fish is done, assemble the tacos by placing some shredded cabbage and avocado on each tortilla, then adding a few pieces of the fried fish on top. Serve with lime wedges.

Coconut-Crusted Mahi-Mahi

Serves: 2

Prep time: 10 minutes / Cook time: 12 minutes

Ingredients:
- 2 mahi-mahi fillets
- 50g all-purpose flour
- 1 large egg, beaten
- 100g unsweetened shredded coconut
- 1/2 tsp sea salt
- 1/4 tsp black pepper
- 1 lime, cut into wedges
- 1 tbsp olive oil

Preparation instructions:

1. Pat the mahi-mahi fillets dry with a paper towel.
2. Set up a breading station: place the flour in one shallow dish, the beaten egg in another dish, and the shredded coconut mixed with the sea salt and black pepper in a third dish.
3. Dip each fillet in the flour, shaking off any excess. Then, dip each fillet in the beaten egg, and finally coat each fillet with the coconut mixture.
4. Preheat the Ninja Dual Zone Air Fryer to 200°C using the "AIR FRY" function.
5. Place the coated mahi-mahi fillets in the crisper plate and spray with olive oil.
6. Select zone 1 and set the time to 6 minutes. Select "AIR FRY" at 200°C and press "START/STOP" to begin cooking.
7. When the timer goes off, carefully flip the fillets and cook for another 6 minutes.
8. Serve the coconut-crusted mahi-mahi with lime wedges on the side.

Lobster Mac and Cheese Bites

Serves: 6

Prep time: 15 minutes / Cook time: 18 minutes

Ingredients:
- 225g elbow macaroni
- 45g unsalted butter
- 45g plain flour
- 350ml whole milk
- 1 tsp garlic powder
- 1 tsp onion powder

- 1 tsp smoked paprika
- Salt and pepper, to taste
- 200g cooked lobster meat, chopped
- 115g sharp cheddar cheese, grated
- 50g panko breadcrumbs
- Cooking spray

Preparation instructions:

1. Preheat the Ninja Dual Zone Air Fryer to 200°C using the "Bake" function.
2. Cook macaroni according to package instructions until al dente. Drain and set aside.
3. In a saucepan, melt butter over medium heat. Add flour and whisk constantly for 1-2 minutes.
4. Gradually whisk in milk until the mixture is smooth. Add garlic powder, onion powder, smoked paprika, salt and pepper.
5. Continue whisking until the mixture thickens and coats the back of a spoon.
6. Remove from heat and stir in the lobster meat and cheddar cheese until fully combined.
7. Add cooked macaroni and stir until well coated.
8. Grease a mini muffin tin with cooking spray. Spoon mac and cheese mixture into each cup.
9. Sprinkle panko breadcrumbs on top of each mac and cheese bite.
10. Place the muffin tin in zone 1 of the Ninja Dual Zone Air Fryer and select "Air Fry" for 8-10 minutes until the tops are golden brown and crispy.
11. Serve immediately.

Salmon Croquettes with Lemon-Dill Sauce

Serves: 4

Prep time: 20 minutes / Cook time: 20 minutes

Ingredients:

- 450g fresh salmon fillet, skin removed
- 60g panko breadcrumbs
- 60g mayonnaise
- 60g chopped green onions
- 1 egg, lightly beaten
- 1 tbsp Dijon mustard
- 1 tsp lemon zest
- 1/4 tsp salt
- 1/4 tsp black pepper
- 120g plain flour
- 120g panko breadcrumbs
- 2 tbsp olive oil

For Lemon-Dill Sauce:

- 120g sour cream
- 2 tbsp fresh dill, chopped
- 1 tbsp lemon juice
- Salt and pepper, to taste

Preparation instructions:

1. Preheat the Ninja Dual Zone Air Fryer to 200°C using the "Roast" function.
2. Cut salmon fillet into small pieces and pulse in a food processor until roughly chopped.
3. In a mixing bowl, combine the salmon, panko breadcrumbs, mayonnaise, green onions, egg, Dijon mustard, lemon zest, salt and black pepper. Mix well.
4. Use a tablespoon to form a mixture into small patties.
5. Place flour and panko breadcrumbs in separate shallow dishes.
6. Dredge each patty in flour, then in egg, and finally in panko breadcrumbs.
7. Brush the air fryer basket with olive oil and place the patties in zone 1 of the Ninja Dual Zone Air Fryer.
8. Roast for 10 minutes on each side or until golden brown and crispy.
9. While salmon croquettes are cooking, mix all ingredients for the lemon-dill sauce in a small bowl and set aside.
10. Serve salmon croquettes hot with lemon-dill sauce on the side.

Shrimp Scampi with Linguine

Serves: 2

Prep time: 10 minutes / Cook time: 20 minutes

Ingredients:

- 225g linguine pasta
- 250g large raw shrimp, peeled and deveined
- 3 cloves garlic, minced
- 60g unsalted butter
- 60g olive oil
- 1/4 tsp red pepper flakes
- 60ml dry white wine
- 60ml chicken or vegetable broth
- 60ml freshly squeezed lemon juice
- Salt and freshly ground black pepper, to taste
- Fresh parsley, chopped for garnish

Preparation instructions:

1. Cook linguine according to package instructions, then drain and set aside.
2. While pasta is cooking, prepare the shrimp: In a bowl, combine the shrimp, minced garlic, and red pepper flakes.
3. In a skillet, melt the butter and olive oil over medium heat. Add the shrimp mixture and sauté for 2-3 minutes, until shrimp turn pink and opaque.
4. Add the white wine, broth, and lemon juice to the skillet, and stir until combined. Let the mixture simmer for 2-3 minutes, or until the sauce has thickened slightly.
5. Add the cooked linguine to the skillet, and toss until pasta is coated in the sauce.
6. Season with salt and freshly ground black pepper, to taste.
7. Serve hot, garnished with chopped parsley.

Tandoori Shrimp Skewers

Serves: 4

Prep time: 15 minutes (plus 30 minutes marinating time) / Cook time: 10 minutes

Ingredients:

- 500g raw jumbo shrimp, peeled and deveined
- 120g plain yoghurt
- 2 tbsp tandoori spice mix

- 2 tbsp lemon juice
- 2 tbsp vegetable oil
- 1 tbsp minced garlic
- 1 tbsp minced ginger
- Salt and freshly ground black pepper, to taste
- Lemon wedges and chopped cilantro, for garnish

Preparation instructions:

1. In a large bowl, combine the yoghurt, tandoori spice mix, lemon juice, vegetable oil, minced garlic, and minced ginger.
2. Add the shrimp to the bowl, and toss until coated in the marinade.
3. Cover and refrigerate for at least 30 minutes (or up to 2 hours) to allow the flavours to meld together.
4. Preheat the Ninja Dual Zone Air Fryer to 200°C.
5. Thread the shrimp on skewers (if using wooden skewers, be sure to soak them in water for at least 30 minutes before using to prevent burning).
6. Place the skewers on the crisper plate in Zone 1 and select "AIR FRY" for 5 minutes.
7. After 5 minutes, carefully remove the crisper plate and flip the skewers over. Return the plate to Zone 1 and select "AIR FRY" for an additional 5 minutes.
8. Once the shrimp are fully cooked and opaque, remove the skewers from the air fryer and season with salt and freshly ground black pepper, to taste.
9. Serve hot, garnished with lemon wedges and chopped cilantro.

Crab Stuffed Mushrooms

Serves: 4

Prep time: 10 minutes / Cook time: 15 minutes

Ingredients:

- 12 large button mushrooms
- 200g fresh crab meat
- 1 small onion, finely chopped

- 1 garlic clove, minced
- 2 tbsp cream cheese
- 1 tbsp chopped fresh parsley
- 1 tbsp lemon juice
- Salt and pepper to taste
- 2 tbsp grated Parmesan cheese
- 1 tbsp olive oil

Preparation instructions:
1. Preheat the Ninja Dual Zone Air Fryer to 180°C on Roast function.
2. Wipe the mushrooms with a damp cloth to remove any dirt. Remove the stems and set aside.
3. In a pan, heat olive oil and sauté onions until soft. Add garlic and cook for another minute.
4. Add crab meat, cream cheese, parsley, lemon juice, salt, and pepper to the pan. Mix well.
5. Spoon the crab mixture into the mushroom caps, and sprinkle with grated Parmesan cheese.
6. Place the stuffed mushrooms onto the crisper plate and air fry in zone 1 at 180°C for 10-15 minutes, or until the cheese is melted and the mushrooms are tender.

Lobster Ravioli with Brown Butter Sauce

Serves: 2

Prep time: 20 minutes / Cook time: 10 minutes

Ingredients:
- 12 fresh or frozen lobster ravioli
- 4 tbsp unsalted butter
- 1 garlic clove, minced
- 1 tbsp chopped fresh sage
- Salt and pepper to taste
- 2 tbsp grated Parmesan cheese

Preparation instructions:
1. Preheat the Ninja Dual Zone Air Fryer to 200°C on Bake function.
2. Cook the ravioli according to the package instructions until al dente.

3. In a pan, melt the butter over medium heat. Add garlic and sage, and cook until the butter turns golden brown and smells nutty.
4. Drain the ravioli and toss them in the brown butter sauce.
5. Transfer the ravioli to the crisper plate and air fry in zone 2 at 200°C for 5 minutes, or until the ravioli are golden brown and crispy.
6. Sprinkle with grated Parmesan cheese and serve immediately.

Cajun Garlic Butter Shrimp

Serves: 2

Prep time: 10 minutes / Cook time: 10 minutes

Ingredients:
- 300g large shrimp, peeled and deveined
- 2 garlic cloves, minced
- 2 tbsp unsalted butter
- 1 tsp Cajun seasoning
- 1/4 tsp smoked paprika
- Salt and pepper, to taste
- Lemon wedges, for serving

Preparation instructions:
1. Preheat the Ninja Dual Zone Air Fryer to 180°C.
2. In a microwave-safe bowl, melt the butter and stir in the garlic, Cajun seasoning, smoked paprika, salt, and pepper.
3. Add the shrimp to the bowl and toss to coat.
4. Arrange the shrimp in a single layer on the crisper plate in zone 1.
5. Select "AIR FRY" at 180°C for 10 minutes.
6. Serve with lemon wedges.

Baked Thai Fish Cakes with Sweet Chili Sauce

Serves: 4

Prep time: 20 minutes / Cook time: 20 minutes

Ingredients:

For the fish cakes:

- 500g white fish fillets, skinless and boneless
- 60g red curry paste
- 1 egg
- 2 tbsp fish sauce
- 2 tbsp brown sugar
- 60g chopped fresh coriander
- 60g chopped green onions
- 60g breadcrumbs
- 2 tbsp vegetable oil
- For the sweet chilli sauce:
- 120ml rice vinegar
- 120g brown sugar
- 60ml water
- 2 tbsp fish sauce
- 2 garlic cloves, minced
- 1-2 red chilli peppers, finely chopped

Preparation instructions:

1. Preheat the Ninja Dual Zone Air Fryer to 200°C.
2. Cut the fish into small pieces and place them in a food processor. Pulse until finely chopped.
3. In a large bowl, combine the fish, red curry paste, egg, fish sauce, brown sugar, coriander, green onions, and breadcrumbs. Mix well.
4. Using your hands, form the mixture into small patties.
5. Brush the patties with vegetable oil and arrange them on the crisper plate in zone 1.
6. Select "AIR FRY" at 200°C for 10 minutes, flip the fish cakes over and cook for another 10 minutes.
7. While the fish cakes are cooking, make the sweet chilli sauce. In a small saucepan, combine the rice vinegar, brown sugar, water, fish sauce, garlic, and chilli peppers. Bring to a boil and simmer for 5 minutes until the sauce thickens.
8. Serve the fish cakes with the sweet chilli sauce on the side.

Blackened Red Snapper with Mango Salsa

Serves: 2

Prep time: 10 minutes / Cook time: 12 minutes

Ingredients:

- 2 (150g each) red snapper fillets
- 1 tbsp paprika
- 1 tsp garlic powder
- 1 tsp onion powder
- 1 tsp dried thyme
- 1 tsp dried oregano
- 1 tsp salt
- 1 tsp black pepper
- 1/4 tsp cayenne pepper
- 2 tsp olive oil
- 1/2 mango, diced
- 1/4 red onion, diced
- 1/2 red bell pepper, diced
- 1 tbsp chopped fresh cilantro
- 1 lime, juiced
- Salt and pepper to taste

Preparation instructions:

1. Preheat the Ninja Dual Zone Air Fryer to 200°C using the broil function.
2. Combine the paprika, garlic powder, onion powder, thyme, oregano, salt, black pepper, and cayenne pepper in a small bowl.
3. Rub the spice mixture evenly over both sides of the red snapper fillets.
4. Place the fillets on the crisper plate and drizzle with olive oil.
5. Place the crisper plate in the air fryer's zone 1 and broil for 6 minutes.
6. Flip the fillets and broil for an additional 6 minutes.
7. While the red snapper is cooking, prepare the mango salsa. In a medium bowl, combine the diced mango, red onion, red bell pepper, cilantro, lime juice, and salt and pepper to taste.
8. Serve the blackened red snapper fillets topped with mango salsa.

Chapter 4: Poultry & Meat Recipes

Szechuan Pepper Steak

Serves: 2

Prep time: 10 minutes / Cook time: 20 minutes

Ingredients:
For the marinade:
- 300g sirloin steak, cut into thin strips
- 2 tbsp cornstarch
- 2 tbsp light soy sauce
- 1 tbsp rice wine or dry sherry
- 1 tsp Szechuan peppercorns, crushed
- 1 tsp brown sugar
- 1 garlic clove, minced
- 1 tsp grated fresh ginger

For the stir-fry:
- 1 tbsp vegetable oil
- 1 red bell pepper, sliced
- 1 green bell pepper, sliced
- 1 onion, sliced
- 2 garlic cloves, minced
- 1 tbsp Szechuan peppercorns, crushed
- Salt and pepper to taste

Preparation instructions:
1. In a large mixing bowl, combine the steak strips with cornstarch, light soy sauce, rice wine or sherry, Szechuan peppercorns, brown sugar, garlic, and ginger. Toss until the steak is evenly coated. Let it sit for 10 minutes.
2. In the meantime, prepare the vegetables. Heat the oil in a frying pan or wok. Add the sliced bell peppers, onion, garlic, and crushed Szechuan peppercorns. Stir-fry for 5-7 minutes, until the vegetables are tender.
3. Using the Ninja Dual Zone Air Fryer, set zone 1 to "AIR FRY" at 200°C for 10 minutes. Once preheated, add the steak strips to the crisper plate, spray with cooking oil, and cook for 5-7 minutes or until desired doneness.
4. Add the cooked steak to the stir-fried vegetables and toss to combine. Season with salt and pepper to taste.
5. Serve hot, garnished with chopped spring onions, and enjoy!
6. Note: For a spicier kick, add more crushed Szechuan peppercorns or sliced chillies to the stir-fry.

Chicken Liver Pate

Serves: 4

Prep time: 10 minutes / Cook time: 40 minutes

Ingredients:
- 250g chicken livers
- 1/2 onion, chopped
- 1 garlic clove, minced
- 1 tsp dried thyme
- 1 bay leaf
- 2 tbsp butter
- 2 tbsp brandy
- 2 tbsp cream
- Salt and pepper to taste

Preparation instructions:
1. Preheat the Ninja Dual Zone Air Fryer to 180°C using the bake function.
2. In a medium saucepan, melt the butter over medium heat. Add the chopped onion and minced garlic and sauté until softened, about 5 minutes.
3. Add the chicken livers, dried thyme, and bay leaf to the saucepan and cook until the livers are browned on the outside but still slightly pink on the inside, about 10 minutes.

4. Remove the bay leaf and transfer the contents of the saucepan to a blender.
5. Add the brandy and cream to the blender and blend until smooth.
6. Season with salt and pepper to taste.
7. Pour the mixture into ramekins and place them on the crisper plate.
8. Place the crisper plate in the air fryer's zone 2 and bake for 20 minutes.
9. Allow the pate to cool to room temperature before serving with toast or crackers.

Braised Lamb Shanks

Serves: 2

Prep time: 15 minutes / Cook time: 3 hours

Ingredients:

- 2 lamb shanks (400g each)
- 1 tbsp vegetable oil
- 1 onion, chopped
- 2 garlic cloves, minced
- 2 carrots, peeled and chopped
- 2 celery sticks, chopped
- 1 bay leaf
- 1 tsp dried thyme
- 1 tsp dried rosemary
- 400ml beef stock
- Salt and black pepper, to taste

Preparation instructions:

1. Preheat your Ninja Dual Zone Air Fryer to 160°C on zone 1.
2. Season the lamb shanks with salt and pepper.
3. Heat the vegetable oil in a large skillet over medium-high heat. Brown the lamb shanks on all sides, about 8 minutes.
4. Remove the lamb shanks from the skillet and set aside.
5. In the same skillet, add the onion, garlic, carrots, and celery. Sauté until the vegetables are softened, about 5 minutes.

6. Add the bay leaf, dried thyme, and dried rosemary. Stir well.
7. Pour in the beef stock and bring to a boil.
8. Transfer the vegetables and stock to the zone 2 basket of your air fryer.
9. Place the lamb shanks on top of the vegetables.
10. Cover the zone 2 basket with foil and place it on top of the zone 1 basket.
11. Select "ROAST" on zone 1 and cook for 3 hours.
12. Remove the foil and transfer the lamb shanks to a serving plate. Spoon the vegetables and juices over the lamb shanks.

Fried Pig Ears

Serves: 4

Prep time: 10 minutes / Cook time: 10 minutes

Ingredients:

- 4 pig ears, cleaned and trimmed
- 1 tsp paprika
- 1 tsp garlic powder
- 1 tsp onion powder
- 1 tsp dried thyme
- 1 tsp dried oregano
- Salt and black pepper, to taste
- 120g plain flour
- 2 eggs, beaten
- 120g panko breadcrumbs
- 2 tbsp vegetable oil

Preparation instructions:

1. Preheat your Ninja Dual Zone Air Fryer to 200°C on zone 1.
2. In a small bowl, mix together the paprika, garlic powder, onion powder, dried thyme, dried oregano, salt, and black pepper.
3. Season the pig ears on both sides with the spice mixture.
4. Place the plain flour in a shallow dish.

5. In another shallow dish, beat the eggs.
6. In a third shallow dish, add the panko breadcrumbs.
7. Dredge each pig ear in the flour, then dip into the egg, and finally coat in the breadcrumbs.
8. Arrange the pig ears on the crisper plate and spray them with vegetable oil.
9. Select "AIR FRY" on zone 1 and cook for 10 minutes, or until golden brown and crispy.
10. Remove the pig ears from the air fryer and let them cool for a few minutes.
11. Slice the pig ears into thin strips and serve with your favourite dipping sauce.

Rosemary and Garlic Pork Tenderloin

Serves: 2-4

Prep time: 10 minutes / Cook time: 20 minutes

Ingredients:

- 1 pork tenderloin (about 500g)
- 2 garlic cloves, minced
- 2 tsp dried rosemary leaves
- 2 tbsp olive oil
- Sea salt and ground black pepper, to taste

Preparation instructions:

1. Preheat the Ninja Dual Zone Air Fryer to 200°C on the Roast function.
2. Combine minced garlic, rosemary leaves, olive oil, salt, and black pepper in a small bowl.
3. Rub the mixture over the pork tenderloin, making sure to coat it evenly.
4. Place the pork tenderloin in zone 1 of the Air Fryer and roast for 10 minutes.
5. After 10 minutes, transfer the pork tenderloin to zone 2 of the Air Fryer and roast for an additional 10 minutes, or until the internal temperature reaches 63°C.

6. Once cooked, remove the pork tenderloin from the Air Fryer and let it rest for a few minutes before slicing and serving.

BBQ Pulled Pork Sliders

Serves: 4-6

Prep time: 10 minutes / Cook time: 35 minutes

Ingredients:

For the pork:
- 1.5 kg pork shoulder
- 2 tbsp smoked paprika
- 1 tbsp garlic powder
- 1 tbsp onion powder
- 1 tbsp brown sugar
- 1 tbsp sea salt
- 1 tsp ground black pepper
- 250ml BBQ sauce

For the sliders:
- 12 slider buns
- 1 small red onion, thinly sliced
- 1 small cucumber, thinly sliced
- 1 avocado, sliced
- 1 tbsp olive oil
- Sea salt and ground black pepper, to taste

Preparation instructions:

1. Preheat the Ninja Dual Zone Air Fryer to 180°C on the Roast function.
2. Combine smoked paprika, garlic powder, onion powder, brown sugar, sea salt, and black pepper in a small bowl.
3. Rub the spice mixture all over the pork shoulder, making sure to coat it evenly.
4. Place the pork shoulder in zone 1 of the Air Fryer and roast for 20 minutes.
5. After 20 minutes, transfer the pork shoulder to zone 2 of the Air Fryer and roast for an additional 15 minutes.
6. Pour the BBQ sauce over the pork shoulder, making sure to coat it evenly.

7. Roast for an additional 10 minutes, or until the internal temperature reaches 71°C.
8. Once cooked, remove the pork shoulder from the Air Fryer and shred it with two forks.
9. In a separate bowl, toss the sliced red onion and cucumber with olive oil, salt, and black pepper.
10. To assemble the sliders, place a generous amount of pulled pork on each bun, top with the sliced avocado and the red onion and cucumber mixture.
11. Serve immediately and enjoy!

Nashville Hot Chicken Sandwiches

Serves: 2

Prep time: 15 minutes / Cook time: 30 minutes

Ingredients:
For the chicken:
- 2 boneless, skinless chicken breasts
- 1 cup buttermilk
- 1 tablespoon hot sauce
- 1 tablespoon paprika
- 1 tablespoon garlic powder
- 1 tablespoon onion powder
- 1 teaspoon cayenne pepper
- 1 teaspoon salt
- 1 cup all-purpose flour
- 1 teaspoon smoked paprika
- 1 teaspoon garlic powder
- 1 teaspoon onion powder
- 1/2 teaspoon cayenne pepper
- 1/2 teaspoon salt
- Oil spray

For the sandwich:
- 2 brioche buns
- 60ml mayonnaise
- 1 tablespoon hot sauce
- 4 pickle slices
- 2 lettuce leaves

Preparation instructions:
1. Preheat the Ninja Dual Zone Air Fryer to 190°C.
2. In a bowl, mix together buttermilk, hot sauce, paprika, garlic powder, onion powder, cayenne pepper, and salt. Add chicken breasts, and coat them with the mixture. Cover and marinate in the refrigerator for at least 1 hour, or overnight.
3. In a shallow dish, mix together flour, smoked paprika, garlic powder, onion powder, cayenne pepper, and salt. Coat chicken breasts in the flour mixture, and shake off any excess flour.
4. Arrange chicken breasts on the crisper plate, and spray with oil. Select zone 1 and pair it with "AIR FRY" for 15 minutes. Flip the chicken over and spray the other side with oil. Select zone 2 and pair it with "AIR FRY" for another 15 minutes.
5. In a small bowl, mix together mayonnaise and hot sauce. Toast brioche buns in the Ninja Dual Zone Air Fryer for 1-2 minutes.
6. Assemble the sandwich by spreading the hot mayo on the bottom bun, and top it with a lettuce leaf, chicken breast, pickles, and the top bun.

Dehydrated Venison Jerky

Serves: 4

Prep time: 10 minutes / Cook time: 4-6 hours

Ingredients:
- 500g venison, thinly sliced
- 120ml soy sauce
- 60ml Worcestershire sauce
- 60g brown sugar
- 1 teaspoon garlic powder
- 1 teaspoon onion powder

- 1/2 teaspoon smoked paprika
- 1/2 teaspoon black pepper

Preparation instructions:

1. In a bowl, mix together soy sauce, Worcestershire sauce, brown sugar, garlic powder, onion powder, smoked paprika, and black pepper. Add venison slices, and coat them with the mixture. Cover and refrigerate for at least 4 hours, or overnight.
2. Preheat the Ninja Dual Zone Air Fryer to 70°C for dehydrating.
3. Remove venison slices from the marinade, and pat them dry using paper towels. Arrange the venison slices on the dehydrator racks.
4. Select zone 1 and pair it with "DEHYDRATE" for 4-6 hours. Check the jerky after 4 hours and remove any pieces that are ready, then continue to dehydrate until the remaining jerky reaches your desired texture.
5. Once the jerky is done, remove it from the dehydrator and let it cool completely. Store in an airtight container at room temperature for up to 2 weeks.

Buffalo Turkey Meatballs

Serves: 4

Prep time: 15 minutes / Cook time: 15 minutes

Ingredients:

- 450g ground turkey
- 60g breadcrumbs
- 60g finely chopped onion
- 1 egg
- 60ml buffalo sauce
- 1/2 tsp garlic powder
- 1/2 tsp salt

- 1/4 tsp black pepper
- 1 tbsp olive oil

Preparation instructions:

1. Preheat your Ninja Dual Zone Air Fryer to 190°C using the AIR FRY function.
2. In a mixing bowl, combine the ground turkey, breadcrumbs, onion, egg, buffalo sauce, garlic powder, salt, and black pepper.
3. Mix well until all ingredients are thoroughly combined.
4. Form the mixture into 16 meatballs.
5. Brush the meatballs with olive oil to help brown and crisp in the air fryer.
6. Arrange the meatballs in a single layer on the crisper plate of the air fryer and place it in zone 1.
7. Select "AIR FRY" at 190°C for 15 minutes.
8. Select "SYNC" followed by the "START/STOP" button.
9. Serve hot with additional buffalo sauce for dipping.

Baked Pesto-Stuffed Chicken Breasts

Serves: 2

Prep time: 15 minutes / Cook time: 25 minutes

Ingredients:

- 2 boneless, skinless chicken breasts
- 60g basil pesto
- 60g grated Parmesan cheese
- 1/4 tsp salt
- 1/4 tsp black pepper
- 1 tbsp olive oil

Preparation instructions:

1. Preheat your Ninja Dual Zone Air Fryer to 190°C using the ROAST function.
2. Cut a pocket horizontally into the thickest part of each chicken breast, being careful not

to cut through the other side.

3. In a small bowl, mix together the pesto, Parmesan cheese, salt, and black pepper.
4. Spoon the mixture evenly into the pockets of each chicken breast.
5. Brush the chicken breasts with olive oil.
6. Arrange the chicken breasts on the crisper plate of the air fryer and place it in zone 2.
7. Select "ROAST" at 190°C for 25 minutes.
8. Select "SYNC" followed by the "START/STOP" button.
9. Serve hot with a side of roasted vegetables or salad.

Baked Bone Marrow

Serves: 4

Prep time: 10 minutes / Cook time: 20 minutes

Ingredients:

- 4 bone marrow pieces (2-3 inches in length)
- 1 tsp sea salt
- 1/2 tsp black pepper
- 1 tsp fresh thyme leaves
- 1 garlic clove, minced
- 4 slices of crusty bread
- 1 tbsp olive oil

Preparation instructions:

1. Preheat the Ninja Dual Zone Air Fryer to 200°C on the "ROAST" function.
2. Place the bone marrow pieces on a baking tray, sprinkle with sea salt, black pepper, thyme leaves, and minced garlic.
3. Roast the bone marrow for 20 minutes in zone 1 of the air fryer.
4. Meanwhile, brush the bread slices with olive oil and place them on the crisper plate in zone 2 of the air fryer.
5..Fry the bread slices for 5 minutes on the "AIR FRY" function until golden brown.
Serve the roasted bone marrow hot with the toasted bread slices.

Smoky Chipotle Beef Ribs

Serves: 4

Prep time: 10 minutes / Cook time: 1 hour

Ingredients:

- 1 kg beef ribs
- 1 tsp smoked paprika
- 1 tsp chipotle chilli powder
- 1 tsp garlic powder
- 1 tsp onion powder
- 1 tsp sea salt
- 1/2 tsp black pepper
- 120ml BBQ sauce
- 2 tbsp honey
- 1 tbsp apple cider vinegar

Preparation instructions:

1. Preheat the Ninja Dual Zone Air Fryer to 180°C on the "ROAST" function.
2. Mix together the smoked paprika, chipotle chilli powder, garlic powder, onion powder, sea salt, and black pepper in a small bowl.
3. Rub the spice mix onto the beef ribs until they are well coated.
4. Place the beef ribs on the crisper plate in zone 1 of the air fryer and cook for 45 minutes.
5. Meanwhile, in a small saucepan, mix together the BBQ sauce, honey, and apple cider vinegar.
6. After 45 minutes, remove the beef ribs from the air fryer and brush them generously with the BBQ sauce mixture.
7. Return the beef ribs to the air fryer and continue cooking for another 15 minutes on the "ROAST" function.
8. Serve the smoky chipotle beef ribs hot with your favourite sides.

Spicy Korean Pork Belly

Serves: 2

Prep time: 10 minutes / Cook time: 30 minutes

Ingredients:

- 400g pork belly slices
- 1 tbsp gochujang (Korean chilli paste)
- 2 tbsp soy sauce
- 2 tbsp honey
- 1 tbsp rice vinegar
- 1 tbsp sesame oil
- 1 tbsp minced garlic
- 1 tbsp minced ginger
- 2 green onions, thinly sliced
- 1 tbsp toasted sesame seeds

Preparation instructions:

1. In a bowl, mix together the gochujang, soy sauce, honey, rice vinegar, sesame oil, garlic, and ginger.
2. Add the pork belly slices to the bowl and toss to coat evenly.
3. Let the pork belly marinate for at least 10 minutes, or up to overnight in the fridge.
4. Preheat the Ninja Dual Zone Air Fryer in "AIRFRYER" mode to 200°C for 5 minutes.
5. Place the pork belly slices on the crisper plate in zone 2 and cook for 15 minutes.
6. After 15 minutes, flip the pork belly slices and cook for another 10-15 minutes until the pork is crispy and fully cooked.
7. Serve with sliced green onions and toasted sesame seeds.

Tandoori Chicken Skewers

Serves: 2

Prep time: 10 minutes / Cook time: 20 minutes

Ingredients:

- 2 boneless chicken breasts, cut into 1-inch pieces
- 120g plain Greek yoghurt
- 2 tbsp tandoori masala
- 1 tbsp minced garlic
- 1 tbsp minced ginger
- 1 tbsp lemon juice
- 1/2 tsp salt
- 1/4 tsp black pepper
- 1 green bell pepper, cut into 1-inch pieces
- 1 red onion, cut into 1-inch pieces

Preparation instructions:

1. In a bowl, mix together the Greek yoghurt, tandoori masala, garlic, ginger, lemon juice, salt, and black pepper.
2. Add the chicken pieces to the bowl and toss to coat evenly.
3. Let the chicken marinate for at least 10 minutes, or up to overnight in the fridge.
4. Preheat the Ninja Dual Zone Air Fryer on "ROAST" mode to 200°C for 5 minutes.
5. Thread the marinated chicken pieces, green bell pepper, and red onion onto skewers.
6. Place the skewers on the crisper plate in zone 1 and cook for 10 minutes.
7. After 10 minutes, flip the skewers and cook for another 10 minutes until the chicken is fully cooked and the vegetables are tender.
8. Serve with rice and naan bread.

Thai Basil Chicken Stir-Fry

Serves: 2

Prep time: 15 minutes / Cook time: 10 minutes

Ingredients:

- 2 chicken breasts, sliced into thin strips
- 1 red bell pepper, sliced into thin strips
- 1 yellow bell pepper, sliced into thin strips
- 1 onion, sliced into thin strips
- 3 garlic cloves, minced
- 1 tsp grated ginger

- 2 tbsp soy sauce
- 2 tbsp oyster sauce
- 1 tbsp fish sauce
- 1 tbsp brown sugar
- 1 tsp cornstarch
- 2 tbsp vegetable oil
- 1 bunch of Thai basil leaves
- Salt and pepper, to taste

Preparation instructions:

1. In a small bowl, whisk together soy sauce, oyster sauce, fish sauce, brown sugar, and cornstarch. Set aside.
2. Select zone 1 and pair it with "STIR-FRY" at 200°C for 5 minutes.
3. Add vegetable oil to the zone 1 cooking pot and let it heat up for 1 minute.
4. Add garlic and ginger, and stir-fry for 30 seconds.
5. Add chicken and stir-fry until browned and cooked through, about 5-7 minutes.
6. Add bell peppers and onion and the sauce and sugar mix, and stir-fry for another 3-5 minutes, until the vegetables are slightly softened.
7. Pour the sauce mixture over the chicken and vegetables, and stir-fry until the sauce thickens and coats everything evenly.
8. Add the Thai basil leaves, and stir-fry for another minute until the leaves are wilted.
9. Serve hot with steamed rice.

Vietnamese Grilled Lemongrass Pork Chops

Serves: 2

Prep time: 10 minutes + 2 hours marinating time / Cook time: 10 minutes

Ingredients:
- 2 pork chops
- 2 stalks lemongrass, finely chopped
- 3 garlic cloves, minced
- 1 tbsp fish sauce
- 1 tbsp soy sauce
- 1 tbsp brown sugar
- 1 tsp sesame oil
- 1/4 tsp black pepper
- 2 tbsp vegetable oil
- Lime wedges, for serving

Preparation instructions:

1. In a small bowl, whisk together lemongrass, garlic, fish sauce, soy sauce, brown sugar, sesame oil, and black pepper.
2. Place pork chops in a shallow dish or ziplock bag, and pour the marinade over them. Turn to coat evenly. Marinate in the refrigerator for at least 2 hours, or overnight.
3. Heat vegetable oil in a grill pan or on a barbecue grill over high heat.
4. Remove pork chops from the marinade, and discard the excess marinade.
5. Grill pork chops for 3-4 minutes on each side, or until cooked through and nicely charred.
6. Serve hot and enjoy!

Jamaican Jerk Pork Tenderloin with Pineapple Salsa

Serves: 4

Prep time: 15 minutes / Cook time: 20 minutes

Ingredients:
- 500g pork tenderloin
- 2 tbsp Jamaican jerk seasoning
- 1 tbsp olive oil
- 1 pineapple, peeled, cored and diced
- 1 red bell pepper, diced
- 1 small red onion, diced
- 2 tbsp chopped fresh coriander
- 1 lime, juiced
- Salt and pepper to taste

Preparation instructions:
1. Preheat the Ninja Dual Zone Air Fryer to 200°C using the "ROAST" function.
2. Rub the pork tenderloin with Jamaican jerk seasoning and olive oil, making sure to coat evenly.
3. Place the pork tenderloin on the crisper plate in Zone 1 and air fry for 20 minutes, or until cooked through and golden brown.
4. While the pork is cooking, mix together the pineapple, red bell pepper, red onion, coriander, lime juice, salt, and pepper to make the salsa.
5. Serve the Jamaican jerk pork tenderloin with the pineapple salsa on the side.

Moroccan-Spiced Chicken Thighs with Apricot Chutney

Serves: 4

Prep time: 15 minutes / Cook time: 20 minutes

Ingredients:
- 8 chicken thighs, bone-in and skin-on
- 2 tbsp Moroccan spice blend
- 1 tbsp olive oil
- 2 tbsp apricot jam
- 1 tbsp white wine vinegar
- 1/4 tsp ground ginger
- 1/4 tsp ground cinnamon
- Salt and pepper to taste

Preparation instructions:
1. Preheat the Ninja Dual Zone Air Fryer to 200°C using the "ROAST" function.
2. Rub the chicken thighs with Moroccan spice blend and olive oil, making sure to coat evenly.
3. Place the chicken thighs on the crisper plate in Zone 1 and air fry for 20 minutes, or until cooked through and crispy.
4. While the chicken is cooking, make the apricot chutney by mixing together the apricot jam, white wine vinegar, ground ginger, ground cinnamon, salt, and pepper in a small bowl.
5. Serve the Moroccan-spiced chicken thighs with the apricot chutney on the side.

Chapter 5: Healthy Vegetables and Sides

Broiled Asparagus with Lemon and Parmesan

Serves: 4

Prep time: 5 minutes / Cook time: 10 minutes

Ingredients:

- 500g asparagus, tough ends removed
- 2 tbsp olive oil
- 1/2 tsp sea salt
- 1/4 tsp black pepper
- 1 lemon, zested and juiced
- 30g grated Parmesan cheese

Preparation instructions:

1. Preheat the Ninja Dual Zone Air Fryer on Broil mode at 200°C.
2. Toss asparagus with olive oil, salt, and black pepper in a mixing bowl.
3. Arrange the asparagus in a single layer on the crisper plate and broil for 5-7 minutes until lightly charred and tender, shaking the basket once halfway through.
4. Transfer the asparagus to a serving platter and sprinkle with lemon zest, lemon juice, and Parmesan cheese.
5. Serve immediately and enjoy!

Dehydrated Vegetable Chips with Sea Salt

Serves: 4

Prep time: 10 minutes / Cook time: 2-3 hours

Ingredients:

- 2 large sweet potatoes
- 2 large carrots
- 2 large beets
- 1 tbsp olive oil
- 1 tsp sea salt

Preparation instructions:

1. Preheat the Ninja Dual Zone Air Fryer on Dehydrate mode at 70°C.
2. Peel and thinly slice the vegetables using a mandolin or a sharp knife.
3. Toss the vegetables with olive oil and sea salt in a mixing bowl.
4. Arrange the vegetable slices in a single layer on the dehydrator rack, making sure to leave enough space between each slice for air circulation.
5. Dehydrate the vegetables for 2-3 hours, or until they are completely dried and crispy.
6. Transfer the vegetable chips to a bowl and serve!

Broiled Brussel Sprouts with Balsamic Glaze

Serves: 4

Prep time: 10 minutes / Cook time: 15 minutes

Ingredients:

- 450g Brussel sprouts, trimmed and halved
- 1 tbsp olive oil
- Sea salt and black pepper, to taste
- 1 tbsp balsamic vinegar
- 1 tsp honey

Preparation instructions:

1. Preheat the Ninja Dual Zone Air Fryer to broil at 220°C.
2. Toss Brussel sprouts with olive oil, salt, and pepper in a bowl.
3. Arrange the Brussel sprouts in a single layer on the crisper plate.

4. Broil in zone 1 for 8 minutes.
5. While the Brussel sprouts are cooking, whisk together balsamic vinegar and honey in a small bowl.
6. Remove the Brussel sprouts from the air fryer and drizzle with balsamic glaze.
7. Return the Brussel sprouts to the air fryer and broil in zone 2 for another 5-7 minutes, or until browned and crispy.
8. Serve immediately.

Broiled Eggplant with Garlic and Tahini Sauce

Serves: 4

Prep time: 15 minutes / Cook time: 15 minutes

Ingredients:

- 1 large eggplant, sliced into rounds
- 1 tbsp olive oil
- Sea salt and black pepper, to taste
- 2 cloves garlic, minced
- 2 tbsp tahini
- 2 tbsp lemon juice
- 60ml water
- 1 tbsp chopped fresh parsley, for garnish

Preparation instructions:

1. Preheat the Ninja Dual Zone Air Fryer to broil at 220°C.
2. Brush eggplant slices with olive oil and season with salt and pepper.
3. Arrange the eggplant slices in a single layer on the crisper plate.
4. Broil in zone 1 for 8 minutes.
5. While the eggplant is cooking, make the garlic and tahini sauce: In a small bowl, whisk together minced garlic, tahini, lemon juice, and water until smooth.
6. Remove the eggplant from the air fryer and arrange on a serving platter.

7. Drizzle the garlic and tahini sauce over the eggplant.
8. Garnish with chopped parsley and serve immediately.

Crispy Brussel Sprouts with Maple Glaze

Serves: 2

Prep time: 10 minutes / Cook time: 20 minutes

Ingredients:

- 300g Brussels sprouts, trimmed and halved
- 1 tbsp olive oil
- Salt and pepper, to taste
- 2 tbsp maple syrup
- 1 tbsp soy sauce
- 1 tbsp balsamic vinegar
- 1 garlic clove, minced
- 1/4 tsp red pepper flakes

Preparation instructions:

1. Preheat the Ninja Dual Zone Air Fryer to 200°C.
2. In a bowl, toss the Brussels sprouts with olive oil, salt, and pepper.
3. Place the Brussels sprouts in the air fryer basket in Zone 1 and select "AIR FRY" for 10 minutes.
4. In the meantime, mix together the maple syrup, soy sauce, balsamic vinegar, garlic, and red pepper flakes in a small bowl.
5. After 10 minutes, open Zone 1 and brush the Brussels sprouts with the maple glaze.
6. Move the air fryer basket to Zone 2 and select "AIR FRY" for another 10 minutes, or until the Brussels sprouts are crispy and caramelised.
7. Serve immediately.

Zucchini Fries with Garlic Aioli

Serves: 2

Prep time: 10 minutes / Cook time: 20 minutes

Ingredients:

- 2 medium zucchinis, cut into fries
- 120g breadcrumbs
- 60g grated parmesan cheese
- 1 tsp garlic powder
- 1/2 tsp salt
- 1/4 tsp black pepper
- 1 egg, beaten
- 1 tbsp olive oil
- 60g mayonnaise
- 1 garlic clove, minced
- 1 tbsp lemon juice
- 1/4 tsp salt

Preparation instructions:

1. Preheat the Ninja Dual Zone Air Fryer to 200°C.
2. In a shallow dish, mix together breadcrumbs, parmesan cheese, garlic powder, salt, and black pepper.
3. Dip zucchini fries into beaten egg, then coat with breadcrumb mixture.
4. Place the coated zucchini fries in the air fryer basket in Zone 1 and select "AIR FRY" for 10 minutes.
5. In the meantime, prepare the garlic aioli by mixing together mayonnaise, minced garlic, lemon juice, and salt in a small bowl.
6. After 10 minutes, open Zone 1 and flip the zucchini fries.
7. Brush with olive oil and move the air fryer basket to Zone 2.
8. Select "AIR FRY" for another 10 minutes or until the zucchini fries are golden brown and crispy.
9. Serve immediately with garlic aioli.

Vegan Spring Rolls with Peanut Dipping Sauce

Serves: 4

Prep time: 20 minutes / Cook time: 10 minutes

Ingredients:

- For the spring rolls:
- 8 rice paper wrappers
- 2 cups thinly sliced cabbage
- 1 large carrot, cut into matchsticks
- 1 red bell pepper, thinly sliced
- 1 small cucumber, seeded and thinly sliced
- 75g fresh mint leaves
- 75g fresh cilantro leaves
- 100g roasted peanuts, roughly chopped
- For the peanut dipping sauce:
- 120g smooth peanut butter
- 80ml warm water
- 2 tbsp soy sauce
- 2 tbsp maple syrup
- 2 cloves garlic, minced
- 1 tsp grated ginger
- 1 lime, juiced

Preparation instructions:

1. Preheat the Ninja Dual Zone Air Fryer on Zone 1 at 180°C for 10 minutes.
2. To make the spring rolls, dip a rice paper wrapper into a bowl of warm water until it softens, about 10 seconds. Place the wrapper onto a damp tea towel.
3. Add a handful of cabbage, carrot, red bell pepper, cucumber, mint, cilantro, and chopped peanuts to the centre of the wrapper.
4. Fold the bottom of the wrapper over the filling, then fold in the sides. Roll the wrapper tightly to enclose the filling. Repeat with the remaining rice paper wrappers and filling.
5. Place the spring rolls onto the crisper plate

and spray with cooking oil. Cook for 8-10 minutes, until the spring rolls are crispy and golden brown.

6. While the spring rolls are cooking, prepare the peanut dipping sauce. In a small bowl, whisk together peanut butter, warm water, soy sauce, maple syrup, garlic, ginger, and lime juice until smooth.

7. Serve the spring rolls with the peanut dipping sauce.

Baked Sweet Potatoes with Sage and Walnuts

Serves: 4

Prep time: 10 minutes / Cook time: 40 minutes

Ingredients:

* 4 medium sweet potatoes, washed and dried
* 2 tbsp olive oil
* 1 tbsp finely chopped fresh sage
* 120g chopped walnuts
* Salt and pepper, to taste

Preparation instructions:

1. Preheat the Ninja Dual Zone Air Fryer on Zone 2 at 200°C for 10 minutes.
2. Prick the sweet potatoes all over with a fork. Rub each potato with olive oil, then season with salt and pepper.
3. Place the sweet potatoes onto the crisper plate and cook for 30-40 minutes, until they are tender and can be easily pierced with a fork.
4. While the sweet potatoes are cooking, toast the chopped walnuts in a dry frying pan until they are lightly browned and fragrant.
5. When the sweet potatoes are cooked, cut a slit down the middle of each potato and sprinkle with fresh sage and toasted walnuts.
6. Serve hot as a side dish or main meal.

Crispy Kale Chips with Smoked Paprika

Serves: 2

Prep time: 5 minutes / Cook time: 8 minutes

Ingredients:

* 150g kale, stems removed and torn into bite-size pieces
* 1 tablespoon olive oil
* 1/2 teaspoon smoked paprika
* Salt, to taste

Preparation instructions:

1. Preheat the Ninja Dual Zone Air Fryer to 160°C using the "AIR FRY" function.
2. In a large bowl, combine the kale, olive oil, smoked paprika, and salt. Toss until the kale is evenly coated.
3. Place the seasoned kale in the crisper plate in a single layer.
4. Select zone 1 and pair it with "AIR FRY" at 160°C for 8 minutes. Select "START/STOP" to begin cooking.
5. After 4 minutes, pause the cooking cycle and use tongs to flip the kale over. Close the lid and continue cooking for the remaining time.
6. Once finished, remove the kale chips from the air fryer and transfer them to a plate. Serve immediately.

Butternut Squash Risotto Cakes

Serves: 4

Prep time: 10 minutes / Cook time: 25 minutes

Ingredients:

* 450g butternut squash, peeled, seeded, and cut into small cubes

- 1 tablespoon olive oil
- Salt and black pepper, to taste
- 1 tablespoon butter
- 1 small onion, finely chopped
- 1 garlic clove, minced
- 200g Arborio rice
- 500ml vegetable stock, heated
- 50g parmesan cheese, grated
- 2 tablespoons breadcrumbs
- 1 tablespoon fresh sage, chopped
- 1 egg, beaten
- 2 tablespoons olive oil

Preparation instructions:

1. Preheat the Ninja Dual Zone Air Fryer to 180°C using the "ROAST" function.
2. In a bowl, toss the butternut squash cubes with olive oil, salt, and black pepper. Spread them out in a single layer on the crisper plate.
3. Select zone 1 and pair it with "ROAST" at 180°C for 20 minutes. Select "START/STOP" to begin cooking.
4. While the butternut squash is roasting, melt the butter in a saucepan over medium heat. Add the onion and garlic, and cook for 3-4 minutes until soft.
5. Add the Arborio rice to the saucepan and cook for 1-2 minutes until toasted.
6. Gradually add the hot vegetable stock to the saucepan, stirring constantly, until the rice is cooked and the liquid is absorbed.
7. Remove the saucepan from the heat and stir in the grated parmesan cheese, breadcrumbs, chopped sage, and beaten egg. Season with salt and black pepper.
8. When the butternut squash is finished roasting, remove it from the air fryer and transfer it to a bowl. Mash it with a fork until smooth.
9. Add the mashed butternut squash to the risotto mixture and stir until well combined.
10. Form the mixture into 8-10 small cakes.
11. Brush the cakes with olive oil and place them on the crisper plate in a single layer.
12. Select zone 2 and pair it with "AIR FRY" at 180°C for 5 minutes. Select "START/STOP" to begin cooking.
13. After 2 minutes, pause the cooking cycle and use tongs to flip the cakes over. Close the lid and continue cooking for the remaining time.
14. Serve the butternut squash risotto cakes as a delicious vegetarian appetisers or a side dish. Enjoy!

Stuffed Artichokes with Parmesan and Herbs

Serves: 4

Prep time: 20 minutes / Cook time: 25 minutes

Ingredients:

- 4 large artichokes
- 2 tablespoons olive oil
- 1 small onion, finely chopped
- 2 cloves garlic, minced
- 120g breadcrumbs
- 60g grated Parmesan cheese
- 1 tablespoon chopped fresh parsley
- 1 tablespoon chopped fresh basil
- Salt and pepper, to taste

Preparation instructions:

1. Preheat the Ninja Dual Zone Air Fryer to 200°C on the "ROAST" function.
2. Prepare the artichokes by removing the tough outer leaves and trimming the tips of the remaining leaves. Cut off the stem so that the artichoke can stand upright. Use a spoon to remove the choke and any small leaves from the centre.
3. Heat the olive oil in a pan over medium heat. Add the onion and garlic, and cook until

softened.

4. Add the breadcrumbs, Parmesan cheese, parsley, basil, salt, and pepper to the pan. Stir until well combined.
5. Stuff the breadcrumb mixture into the centre of each artichoke, pressing down to pack it in.
6. Place the stuffed artichokes in the air fryer basket, standing upright. Air fry for 25 minutes or until the artichokes are tender and the breadcrumbs are golden brown.
7. Serve hot.

Vegan Falafel Patties

Serves: 4

Prep time: 15 minutes / Cook time: 20 minutes

Ingredients:

- 480g cooked chickpeas, drained and rinsed
- 1 small onion, chopped
- 3 cloves garlic, minced
- 60g fresh parsley leaves
- 60g fresh cilantro leaves
- 1 teaspoon ground cumin
- 1/2 teaspoon ground coriander
- 1/4 teaspoon cayenne pepper
- 1/2 teaspoon salt
- 1/4 teaspoon black pepper
- 1 tablespoon lemon juice
- 2 tablespoons all-purpose flour
- 2 tablespoons olive oil

Preparation instructions:

1. Preheat the Ninja Dual Zone Air Fryer to 200°C on the "FRY" function.
2. Place the chickpeas, onion, garlic, parsley, cilantro, cumin, coriander, cayenne pepper, salt, black pepper, and lemon juice in a food processor. Pulse until well combined, but still slightly chunky.
3. Transfer the mixture to a bowl and add the flour. Stir until well combined.

4. Use a tablespoon to form the mixture into 8 patties.
5. Brush both sides of each patty with olive oil.
6. Place the patties in the air fryer basket and air fry for 10 minutes.
7. Flip the patties over and air fry for an additional 10 minutes or until golden brown and crispy.
8. Serve hot with your favourite dipping sauce.

Herbed Hasselback Potatoes

Serves: 4

Prep time: 15 minutes / Cook time: 35 minutes

Ingredients:

- 4 large potatoes
- 2 tbsp olive oil
- 1 tbsp chopped fresh thyme leaves
- 1 tbsp chopped fresh rosemary leaves
- 2 cloves garlic, minced
- 1 tsp sea salt
- 1/2 tsp ground black pepper
- 30g grated Parmesan cheese

Preparation instructions:

1. Preheat the Ninja Dual Zone Air Fryer to 200°C.
2. Slice potatoes into thin, evenly spaced slices but not all the way through.
3. In a small mixing bowl, combine olive oil, thyme, rosemary, garlic, salt, and black pepper.
4. Brush the seasoned oil mixture over the potatoes, making sure to get into the slices.
5. Place the prepared potatoes in the crisper plate and insert it into zone 1.
6. Select zone 1 and pair it with "AIR FRY" at 200°C for 25 minutes.
7. After 25 minutes, remove the crisper plate and sprinkle Parmesan cheese over the potatoes.

8. Place the crisper plate back into zone 1 and select "BROIL" for 5-10 minutes, or until the cheese is melted and bubbly.
9. Serve hot.

Parmesan-Roasted Asparagus

Serves: 4

Prep time: 5 minutes / Cook time: 8 minutes

Ingredients:

- 450g asparagus spears, trimmed
- 2 tbsp olive oil
- 1/2 tsp sea salt
- 1/4 tsp ground black pepper
- 30g grated Parmesan cheese

Preparation instructions:

1. Preheat the Ninja Dual Zone Air Fryer to 200°C.
2. In a small mixing bowl, toss the asparagus with olive oil, salt, and black pepper.
3. Arrange the seasoned asparagus on the crisper plate and insert it into zone 1.
4. Select zone 1 and pair it with "ROAST" at 200°C for 8 minutes.
5. After 8 minutes, remove the crisper plate and sprinkle Parmesan cheese over the asparagus.
6. Place the crisper plate back into zone 1 and select "BROIL" for 2-3 minutes, or until the cheese is melted and bubbly.
7. Serve hot.

Turmeric-Roasted Chickpeas

Serves: 4

Prep time: 5 minutes / Cook time: 20 minutes

Ingredients:

- 400g can chickpeas, drained and rinsed
- 1 tablespoon olive oil
- 1 teaspoon ground turmeric
- 1/2 teaspoon smoked paprika
- 1/2 teaspoon garlic powder
- Sea salt, to taste

Preparation instructions:

1. Preheat the Ninja Dual Zone Air Fryer to 200°C using the ROAST function.
2. In a bowl, toss the chickpeas with the olive oil, turmeric, smoked paprika, garlic powder, and salt until well coated.
3. Spread the chickpeas evenly on the crisper plate in Zone 1.
4. Roast the chickpeas for 20 minutes, shaking the crisper plate halfway through the cooking time.
5. Serve hot as a snack or add them to your favourite salad for some crunch.

Miso-Glazed Eggplant

Serves: 2

Prep time: 10 minutes / Cook time: 15 minutes

Ingredients:

- 1 medium-sized eggplant, sliced into 1/2-inch thick rounds
- 1 tablespoon olive oil
- 1 tablespoon white miso paste
- 1 tablespoon rice vinegar
- 1 tablespoon honey
- 1 garlic clove, minced
- Sesame seeds, for garnish

Preparation instructions:

1. Preheat the Ninja Dual Zone Air Fryer to 200°C using the ROAST function.
2. In a small bowl, whisk together the miso paste, rice vinegar, honey, and garlic until well combined.
3. Brush both sides of the eggplant slices with olive oil and place them in Zone 1 on the

crisper plate.

4. Roast the eggplant slices for 5 minutes, flip them, and roast for an additional 5 minutes.

5. Brush the miso glaze on the eggplant slices and return them to Zone 1 for another 5 minutes.

6. Sprinkle sesame seeds over the eggplant slices and serve hot as a side dish or as a main with steamed rice.

Stuffed Acorn Squash with Wild Rice and Mushrooms

Serves: 4

Prep time: 15 minutes / Cook time: 50 minutes

Ingredients:

- 2 acorn squashes, halved and seeds removed
- 240g wild rice, cooked
- 240g mushrooms, sliced
- 1/2 onion, chopped
- 1 garlic clove, minced
- 1 tbsp olive oil
- 1 tsp dried thyme
- Salt and pepper, to taste
- 60g grated Parmesan cheese

Preparation instructions:

1. Preheat the Ninja Dual Zone Air Fryer to 200°C using the "ROAST" function.

2. In a frying pan, heat the olive oil over medium heat. Add the onions and garlic, and sauté until softened.

3. Add the mushrooms and thyme, and cook for another 5 minutes.

4. In a large bowl, combine the cooked wild rice and the mushroom mixture. Season with salt and pepper to taste.

5. Stuff the acorn squash halves with the wild rice mixture and place them on the crisper plate.

6. Sprinkle the grated Parmesan cheese over the stuffed acorn squash halves.

7. Select zone 2 and pair it with "ROAST" at 200°C for 40-50 minutes or until the squash is tender and the cheese is melted and golden.

Spicy Baked Sweet Potato Wedges

Serves: 4

Prep time: 10 minutes / Cook time: 18 minutes

Ingredients:

- 2 large sweet potatoes, cut into wedges
- 2 tbsp olive oil
- 1 tsp smoked paprika
- 1 tsp garlic powder
- 1/2 tsp cumin
- 1/2 tsp cayenne pepper
- Salt and pepper, to taste

Preparation instructions:

1. Preheat the Ninja Dual Zone Air Fryer to 200°C using the "AIR FRY" function.

2. In a large bowl, toss the sweet potato wedges with olive oil.

3. In a small bowl, mix together the smoked paprika, garlic powder, cumin, cayenne pepper, salt, and pepper.

4. Sprinkle the spice mixture over the sweet potato wedges and toss to coat evenly.

5. Arrange the seasoned sweet potato wedges on the crisper plate.

6. Select zone 1 and pair it with "AIR FRY" at 200°C for 15-18 minutes or until the sweet potato wedges are crispy on the outside and tender on the inside.

7. Serve hot with your favourite dipping sauce.

Chapter 6: Fast and Easy Everyday Favourites

Quails Eggs in Yorkshire Puddings

Serves: 4

Prep time: 15 minutes / Cook time: 25 minutes

Ingredients:

- 8 quail eggs
- 4 tsp wholegrain mustard
- 100g plain flour
- 1/4 tsp salt
- 2 eggs
- 100ml milk
- Vegetable oil, for greasing

Preparation instructions:

1. Preheat the Ninja Dual Zone Air Fryer to 200°C using the "BAKE" function.
2. Grease the muffin cups with vegetable oil.
3. In a mixing bowl, sift the flour and salt together.
4. In a separate bowl, whisk the eggs and milk together until well-combined.
5. Gradually pour the egg mixture into the flour mixture and whisk until a smooth batter is formed.
6. Divide the batter evenly among the muffin cups.
7. Carefully place a quail egg in each cup and add 1/2 tsp of wholegrain mustard on top.
8. Bake the Yorkshire puddings in zone 1 of the Air Fryer for 25 minutes until risen and golden.
9. Serve hot.

Crispy Parmesan Chicken Tenders

Serves: 4

Prep time: 15 minutes / Cook time: 15 minutes

Ingredients:

- 450g chicken breast, cut into thin strips
- 1 tsp garlic powder
- 1 tsp onion powder
- 1 tsp dried thyme
- 1 tsp dried basil
- 1/2 tsp paprika
- 1/4 tsp salt
- 1/4 tsp black pepper
- 60g plain flour
- 2 eggs, beaten
- 100g panko breadcrumbs
- 50g grated Parmesan cheese
- 2 tbsp olive oil

Preparation instructions:

1. Preheat the Ninja Dual Zone Air Fryer to 200°C using the "AIR FRY" function.
2. In a mixing bowl, combine the garlic powder, onion powder, dried thyme, dried basil, paprika, salt, and black pepper.
3. Place the flour in a shallow dish and season with the spice mixture.
4. In a separate shallow dish, beat the eggs.
5. In a third shallow dish, mix the panko breadcrumbs and Parmesan cheese.
6. Dip the chicken strips in the seasoned flour, then in the beaten eggs, and finally, in the breadcrumb mixture, pressing the mixture onto the chicken to coat evenly.
7. Brush the chicken strips with olive oil.
8. Arrange the chicken strips on the crisper plate in zone 1 of the Air Fryer and fry for 15 minutes, flipping halfway through, until golden and crispy.
9. Serve hot with your favourite dipping sauce.

Vegetarian Quesadillas with Avocado Cream

Serves: 2

Prep time: 10 minutes / Cook time: 8 minutes

Ingredients:

- For the quesadillas:
- 4 flour tortillas
- 1 can of black beans, rinsed and drained
- 1 red bell pepper, diced
- 1 small onion, diced
- 1 tsp ground cumin
- 1 tsp paprika
- 1 tsp garlic powder
- 1 tsp salt
- 1/2 tsp black pepper
- 1 tbsp olive oil
- 100g cheddar cheese, grated
- For the avocado cream:
- 1 ripe avocado, pitted and peeled
- 120g sour cream
- Juice of 1/2 lime
- Salt and pepper to taste

Preparation instructions:

1. Preheat the Ninja Dual Zone Air Fryer to 180°C in zone 1 and zone 2.
2. In a pan, heat the olive oil over medium-high heat. Add the red bell pepper and onion, and sauté for 3-4 minutes, until they begin to soften.
3. Add the black beans, ground cumin, paprika, garlic powder, salt, and black pepper to the pan, and stir to combine. Cook for 2-3 minutes, until heated through.
4. To make the avocado cream, combine the avocado, sour cream, lime juice, salt, and pepper in a blender or food processor. Blend until smooth and creamy.
5. To assemble the quesadillas, lay two tortillas on a flat surface. Divide the black bean mixture between the two tortillas, spreading it evenly over the surface. Sprinkle the grated cheese on top of the black bean mixture. Top each tortilla with another

tortilla, pressing down gently to seal.
6. Place the quesadillas on the crisper plate of zone 1, and cook for 4 minutes. Flip the quesadillas over, and cook for an additional 4 minutes, until the cheese is melted and the tortillas are crispy.
7. Serve the quesadillas with a dollop of avocado cream on top.

Cheesy Beef Empanadas

Serves: 4

Prep time: 20 minutes / Cook time: 16 minutes

Ingredients:

- For the empanadas:
- 300g beef mince
- 1 small onion, diced
- 1 red bell pepper, diced
- 2 cloves of garlic, minced
- 1 tsp ground cumin
- 1 tsp smoked paprika
- 1/2 tsp salt
- 1/4 tsp black pepper
- 1 tbsp olive oil
- 200g cheddar cheese, grated
- 1 egg, beaten
- 1 tbsp water
- 2 sheets of ready-made shortcrust pastry
- 1 tsp chilli powder

Preparation instructions:

1. Preheat your Ninja Dual Zone Air Fryer to 180°C.
2. In a large skillet, brown the ground beef with the onion and garlic until the beef is fully cooked and the onion is tender.
3. Add the chilli powder, cumin, salt, and pepper to the skillet and stir to combine.
4. Add the shredded cheddar cheese to the skillet and stir until the cheese is melted and everything is well combined.

5. On a flat surface, unroll the crescent roll dough and separate into triangles.
6. Spoon a heaping tablespoon of the beef mixture onto the centre of each triangle.
7. Fold the dough over the beef to create a triangle shape and pinch the edges to seal.
8. Brush each empanada with the beaten egg.
9. Place the empanadas in the air fryer and cook for 10-12 minutes or until the crust is golden brown and crispy.
10. Once cooked, remove the empanadas from the air fryer and allow them to cool for a few minutes before serving.

Spinach and Feta Stuffed Chicken Breasts

Serves: 2

Prep time: 15 minutes / Cook time: 25 minutes

Ingredients:

- 2 boneless, skinless chicken breasts
- 300g fresh spinach leaves, chopped
- 120g crumbled feta cheese
- 2 cloves garlic, minced
- 1/4 teaspoon dried oregano
- 1/4 teaspoon dried basil
- Salt and pepper, to taste
- 1 tablespoon olive oil

Preparation instructions:

1. Preheat your Ninja Dual Zone Air Fryer to 180°C.
2. Using a sharp knife, cut a slit in each chicken breast to create a pocket.
3. In a mixing bowl, combine the spinach, feta cheese, garlic, oregano, basil, salt, and pepper.
4. Stuff the chicken breasts with the spinach and feta mixture.
5. Rub the chicken breasts with olive oil and season with additional salt and pepper.

6. Place the stuffed chicken breasts in the air fryer basket.
7. Select zone 1 and pair it with "AIR FRY" at 180°C for 12 minutes. Select zone 2 and pair it with "AIR FRY" at 180°C for 25 minutes. Select "SYNC" followed by the "START/ STOP" button.
8. Once the cooking time is complete, remove the chicken breasts from the air fryer and let them rest for a few minutes before serving.

Cajun Fish Tacos with Cilantro Lime Sauce

Serves: 2

Prep time: 15 minutes / Cook time: 10 minutes

Ingredients:

For the fish tacos:
- 2 white fish fillets (such as cod or tilapia)
- 1 tablespoon Cajun seasoning
- Salt and pepper, to taste
- 2 tablespoons olive oil
- 4 small flour or corn tortillas
- 240g shredded cabbage
- 1 avocado, sliced
- 1 lime, cut into wedges

For the cilantro lime sauce:
- 120g plain Greek yoghurt
- 60g chopped fresh cilantro
- Juice of 1 lime
- Salt and pepper, to taste

Preparation instructions:

1. Preheat your Ninja Dual Zone Air Fryer to 200°C.
2. Season the fish fillets with Cajun seasoning, salt, and pepper.
3. Brush the fish fillets with olive oil and place them in the air fryer basket.
4. Select zone 1 and pair it with "AIR FRY" at 200°C for 5 minutes. Select zone 2 and pair

it with "AIR FRY" at 200°C for 10 minutes. Select "SYNC" followed by the "START/ STOP" button.

5. While the fish is cooking, make the cilantro lime sauce by mixing together the Greek yoghurt, cilantro, lime juice, salt, and pepper in a small bowl.
6. Warm the tortillas in the air fryer for 1-2 minutes.
7. To assemble the tacos, place the fish on the warm tortillas and top with shredded cabbage, sliced avocado, and a drizzle of the cilantro lime sauce. Serve with lime wedges on the side.

Pork Carnitas Bowls with Avocado and Lime

Serves: 4

Prep time: 10 minutes / Cook time: 30 minutes

Ingredients:

For the Pork Carnitas:
- 1 kg boneless pork shoulder
- 1 tsp ground cumin
- 1 tsp smoked paprika
- 1 tsp garlic powder
- 1 tsp dried oregano
- 1/2 tsp sea salt
- 1/2 tsp black pepper
- 2 tbsp olive oil

For the Rice:
- 200g white rice
- 400ml chicken stock
- 1 tsp ground cumin
- 1 tsp garlic powder
- 1/2 tsp sea salt
- For the Bowl:
- 1 ripe avocado, sliced
- 1 lime, cut into wedges
- Fresh cilantro, chopped

- Sour cream, to serve

Preparation instructions:

1. Preheat the Ninja Dual Zone Air Fryer to 200°C on zone 1.
2. Mix the ground cumin, smoked paprika, garlic powder, dried oregano, sea salt, and black pepper in a small bowl.
3. Rub the spice mixture over the pork shoulder.
4. Place the pork shoulder on the crisper plate and drizzle with olive oil.
5. Select zone 1 and pair it with the "ROAST" function for 30 minutes.
6. Remove the pork from the Ninja Dual Zone Air Fryer and shred the meat.
7. Meanwhile, in a medium-sized saucepan, combine the white rice, chicken stock, ground cumin, garlic powder, and sea salt. Bring the mixture to a boil, reduce the heat to low, cover, and simmer for 15-20 minutes or until the rice is cooked through.
8. To assemble the bowls, place a generous scoop of cooked rice in each bowl, followed by a portion of the shredded pork.
9. Top the pork with sliced avocado, fresh cilantro, and a squeeze of lime juice. Serve with sour cream on the side.

Buffalo Cauliflower Wings with Blue Cheese Dip

Serves: 4

Prep time: 15 minutes / Cook time: 25 minutes

Ingredients:

For the Cauliflower Wings:
- 1 medium-sized cauliflower, cut into bite-sized florets
- 100g plain flour
- 1 tsp garlic powder
- 1 tsp onion powder

- 1/2 tsp smoked paprika
- 1/4 tsp sea salt
- 1/4 tsp black pepper
- 120ml milk
- 120ml water
- 100g panko breadcrumbs
- 75ml buffalo sauce
- For the Blue Cheese Dip:
- 100g blue cheese, crumbled
- 120ml sour cream
- 60ml mayonnaise
- 1 tbsp lemon juice
- 1/4 tsp sea salt
- 1/4 tsp black pepper

Preparation instructions:

1. Preheat the Ninja Dual Zone Air Fryer to 200°C on zone 1.
2. In a large mixing bowl, whisk together the plain flour, garlic powder, onion powder, smoked paprika, sea salt, and black pepper.
3. In a separate bowl, whisk together the milk and water.
4. Add the cauliflower florets to the flour mixture, and toss to coat.
5. Dip the cauliflower florets into the milk mixture, then roll them in the panko breadcrumbs to coat.
6. Place the breaded cauliflower florets on the crisper plate and spray with cooking oil.
7. Select zone 1 and pair it with the "AIR FRY" function for 20 minutes.
8. Meanwhile, prepare the blue cheese dip by combining the blue cheese, sour cream, mayonnaise, lemon juice, sea salt, and black pepper in a bowl.
9. After 20 minutes, remove the cauliflower from the Ninja Dual Zone Air Fryer and toss in buffalo sauce.
10. Serve the buffalo cauliflower wings hot, with the blue cheese dip on the side.

Vietnamese Pork and Vermicelli Bowls

Serves: 4

Prep time: 10 minutes / Cook time: 20 minutes

Ingredients:

- For the pork:
- 450g pork tenderloin, sliced into thin pieces
- 2 garlic cloves, minced
- 2 tbsp fish sauce
- 1 tbsp soy sauce
- 1 tbsp honey
- 1 tsp paprika
- 1/4 tsp black pepper
- 1 tbsp vegetable oil
- For the bowls:
- 250g vermicelli noodles
- 2 medium carrots, julienned
- 1/2 cucumber, thinly sliced
- 120g fresh cilantro, chopped
- 60g roasted peanuts, chopped
- 2 tbsp vegetable oil
- 1 lime, cut into wedges
- Sriracha, to taste

Preparation instructions:

1. Preheat zone 1 of your Ninja Dual Zone Air Fryer to 200°C on the "Roast" function.
2. In a medium bowl, whisk together garlic, fish sauce, soy sauce, honey, paprika, black pepper, and vegetable oil. Add pork slices and marinate for at least 10 minutes.
3. In another bowl, soak vermicelli noodles in hot water for 10 minutes until tender. Drain and rinse with cold water.
4. Toss carrots and cucumber with 2 tablespoons of vegetable oil.
5. Arrange pork slices on zone 1 and cook for 10-12 minutes, or until browned and cooked through.
6. In zone 2, cook the vegetable mixture for

8-10 minutes or until tender and lightly browned.
7. Divide the noodles into four bowls, top with cooked pork, vegetables, cilantro, and chopped peanuts.
8. Serve with lime wedges and Sriracha.

Baked Panko-Crusted Crab Cakes

Serves: 4

Prep time: 10 minutes / Cook time: 20 minutes

Ingredients:
- 450g lump crabmeat, drained and picked over
- 60g mayonnaise
- 60g panko breadcrumbs
- 2 tbsp chopped fresh parsley
- 1 tbsp Dijon mustard
- 1 egg, lightly beaten
- 1 tbsp Worcestershire sauce
- 1 tsp Old Bay seasoning
- Salt and pepper, to taste
- 1 tbsp vegetable oil

Preparation instructions:
1. Preheat zone 1 of your Ninja Dual Zone Air Fryer to 200°C on the "Bake" function.
2. In a large bowl, combine crabmeat, mayonnaise, 1/4 of the panko breadcrumbs, parsley, Dijon mustard, egg, Worcestershire sauce, Old Bay seasoning, salt, and pepper.
3. Form the mixture into 8 crab cakes and coat with remaining panko breadcrumbs.
4. Arrange the crab cakes on zone 1 and bake for 10-12 minutes, or until golden brown and cooked through.
5. Serve hot with your favourite dipping sauce.

Chicken Fajitas with Bell Peppers and Onions

Serves: 4

Prep time: 10 minutes / Cook time: 20 minutes

Ingredients:
- 4 boneless, skinless chicken breasts, sliced
- 1 red bell pepper, sliced
- 1 yellow bell pepper, sliced
- 1 green bell pepper, sliced
- 1 large onion, sliced
- 2 cloves garlic, minced
- 2 tbsp olive oil
- 1 tsp chilli powder
- 1 tsp ground cumin
- 1 tsp paprika
- 1/2 tsp salt
- 1/4 tsp black pepper
- 8 small flour tortillas
- Lime wedges, for serving

Preparation instructions:
1. In a large bowl, combine the chicken, bell peppers, onion, garlic, olive oil, chilli powder, cumin, paprika, salt, and black pepper. Toss until well coated.
2. Preheat the Ninja Dual Zone Air Fryer on "AIR FRY" at 200°C for 5 minutes.
3. Divide the chicken and vegetable mixture evenly between the two zones of the air fryer basket.
4. Air fry in Zone 1 at 200°C for 10 minutes, stirring occasionally.
5. While the chicken and vegetables are cooking, wrap the tortillas in foil and place them in Zone 2. Air fry at 200°C for 5 minutes, or until heated through.
6. Serve the chicken and vegetable mixture in the warm tortillas, with lime wedges on the side.

Hawaiian Teriyaki Chicken Skewers with Pineapple Salsa

Serves: 4

Prep time: 15 minutes / Cook time: 10 minutes

Ingredients:

- 4 boneless, skinless chicken breasts, cut into 1-inch cubes
- 120ml teriyaki sauce
- 2 tbsp honey
- 1 tbsp vegetable oil
- 1 tsp garlic powder
- 1/2 tsp ground ginger
- 1/4 tsp black pepper
- 1/2 pineapple, peeled and cut into 1-inch cubes
- 1 small red onion, cut into 1-inch cubes
- 1 red bell pepper, cut into 1-inch cubes
- 1 yellow bell pepper, cut into 1-inch cubes
- Salt, to taste
- Lime wedges, for serving

Preparation instructions:

1. In a large bowl, whisk together the teriyaki sauce, honey, vegetable oil, garlic powder, ginger, and black pepper. Add the chicken and toss until well coated. Marinate for at least 15 minutes.
2. Preheat the Ninja Dual Zone Air Fryer on "BROIL" at 200°C for 5 minutes.
3. Thread the chicken, pineapple, red onion, red bell pepper, and yellow bell pepper onto skewers, alternating between the ingredients.
4. Season the skewers with salt, to taste.
5. Place the skewers in Zone 1 of the air fryer basket and air fry for 5 minutes, then turn the skewers and air fry for another 5 minutes, or until the chicken is cooked through and the vegetables are tender.
6. While the skewers are cooking, prepare the pineapple salsa by mixing together the remaining pineapple, red onion, red bell pepper, yellow bell pepper, and lime juice in a bowl.
7. Serve the skewers with the pineapple salsa and lime wedges on the side.

Indian Butter Chicken with Naan Bread

Serves: 2

Prep time: 15 minutes / Cook time: 25 minutes

Ingredients:

For the chicken:
- 2 boneless, skinless chicken breasts, cut into bite-sized pieces
- 1 tbsp garam masala
- 1 tsp ground cumin
- 1 tsp ground coriander
- 1/2 tsp turmeric
- 1/4 tsp cayenne pepper
- 1/4 tsp ground cinnamon
- 1/4 tsp ground cardamom
- 1/2 tsp salt
- 1/4 tsp black pepper
- 1 tbsp vegetable oil
- 60g unsalted butter
- 1 small onion, finely chopped
- 1 tbsp grated ginger
- 2 garlic cloves, minced
- 240g tomato puree
- 120g heavy cream
- 60g chopped fresh cilantro

For the naan bread:
- 240g plain flour
- 1/2 tsp baking powder
- 1/4 tsp baking soda
- 1/2 tsp salt
- 120g plain Greek yoghurt
- 1 tbsp vegetable oil

Preparation instructions:

For the chicken:

1. In a small bowl, mix together the garam masala, cumin, coriander, turmeric, cayenne pepper, cinnamon, cardamom, salt, and black pepper.
2. Heat the vegetable oil in a large skillet over medium-high heat. Add the chicken and sprinkle with the spice mixture. Cook until browned, stirring occasionally, about 5 minutes.
3. Add the butter to the skillet and stir until melted. Add the onion, ginger, and garlic, and cook until the onion is translucent, about 3 minutes.
4. Stir in the tomato puree and cream. Bring to a simmer and cook for 10 minutes, until the sauce has thickened.
5. Sprinkle it with cilantro and serve with naan bread.

For the naan bread:

1. In a medium bowl, whisk together the flour, baking powder, baking soda, and salt.
2. In a small bowl, whisk together the yoghurt and oil. Add the yoghurt mixture to the flour mixture and stir until a soft dough forms.
3. Knead the dough on a floured surface for 2-3 minutes, until smooth.
4. Divide the dough into 4 pieces and roll each piece into a circle about 1/4 inch thick.
5. Preheat the Ninja Dual Zone Air Fryer on zone 1 to 200°C. Place the naan bread in the basket and cook for 2-3 minutes, until lightly browned and puffy. Flip and cook for another 1-2 minutes. Serve warm.

Sesame-Ginger Tofu Bowls with Bok Choy and Shiitake Mushrooms

Serves: 2

Prep time: 20 minutes / Cook time: 20 minutes

Ingredients:

For the tofu:

- 350g firm tofu, drained and cut into cubes
- 2 tbsp soy sauce
- 1 tbsp honey
- 1 tbsp sesame oil
- 2 garlic cloves, minced
- 1 tbsp grated ginger
- 1 tbsp cornstarch
- 1 tbsp sesame seeds

For the bowls:

- 150g brown rice, cooked
- 2 bok choy, chopped
- 150g shiitake mushrooms, sliced
- 1 red bell pepper, sliced
- 1 tbsp soy sauce
- 1 tbsp honey
- 1 tbsp sesame oil
- 1 tbsp grated ginger
- 1 garlic clove, minced
- 1 tbsp cornstarch
- 2 tbsp vegetable oil

Preparation instructions:

1. Preheat the Ninja Dual Zone Air Fryer to 200°C in zone 2 using the "AIR FRY" function.
2. In a medium bowl, mix together the soy sauce, honey, sesame oil, garlic, and ginger. Add the tofu cubes and toss to coat.
3. In a small bowl, mix the cornstarch and sesame seeds. Add the tofu and toss until coated.
4. Arrange the tofu on the crisper plate in zone 2 and cook for 10 minutes.
5. While the tofu is cooking, heat the vegetable oil in a frying pan over medium-high heat. Add the bok choy, shiitake mushrooms, and red bell pepper. Cook for 5 minutes.
6. In a small bowl, mix together the soy sauce, honey, sesame oil, garlic, ginger, and cornstarch. Add the mixture to the pan with

the vegetables and cook for an additional 3 minutes.

7. Divide the cooked brown rice between two bowls. Add the cooked vegetables and sesame-ginger tofu. Serve hot.

8. Enjoy your delicious Sesame-Ginger Tofu Bowls with Bok Choy and Shiitake Mushrooms cooked with the Ninja Dual Zone Air Fryer!

Mushroom Risotto Balls

Serves: 4-6

Prep time: 20 minutes / Cook time: 25 minutes

Ingredients:

- 240g Arborio rice
- 720ml vegetable broth
- 1/2 onion, diced
- 2 garlic cloves, minced
- 120g grated parmesan cheese
- 120g dry breadcrumbs
- 120g chopped mushrooms
- 2 tablespoons olive oil
- 1 teaspoon dried thyme
- 1/2 teaspoon salt
- 1/4 teaspoon black pepper
- 120g all-purpose flour
- 1 egg, beaten
- Cooking spray

Preparation instructions:

1. In a medium saucepan, heat the vegetable broth over low heat and keep it simmering.

2. In a separate large saucepan, heat the olive oil over medium heat. Add the onion and garlic and cook until softened, about 3-4 minutes.

3. Add the Arborio rice to the pan and stir to coat it in the oil. Cook for 1-2 minutes until the rice is slightly toasted.

4. Add 1/2 of the simmering broth to the rice and stir constantly until it is absorbed. Continue adding 100 ml of broth at a time, stirring constantly and waiting until each addition is absorbed before adding more.

5. After about 20 minutes of stirring and adding broth, the rice should be tender and creamy. Remove the pan from the heat and stir in the parmesan cheese, mushrooms, thyme, salt, and black pepper.

6. Transfer the risotto to a bowl and let it cool for 10-15 minutes.

7. Once the risotto has cooled, use your hands to form small balls (about 1 1/2 inch in diameter) and place them on a baking sheet lined with parchment paper.

8. In a small bowl, whisk together the egg and 1 tablespoon of water. Place the flour, egg mixture, and breadcrumbs in three separate shallow dishes.

9. Roll each risotto ball in the flour, then dip it in the egg mixture, and finally roll it in the breadcrumbs, making sure it is fully coated.

10. Preheat the Ninja Dual Zone Air Fryer on zone 1 to 190°C and on zone 2 to 200°C.

11. Lightly coat the air fryer basket with cooking spray. Place the risotto balls in the basket, making sure they are not touching each other. Spray the tops of the balls with cooking spray.

12. Select zone 1 and pair it with "AIR FRY" at 190°C for 10 minutes. Then, select zone 2 and pair it with "AIR FRY" at 200°C for 15 minutes.

13. Carefully remove the risotto balls from the air fryer and let them cool for a few minutes before serving.

14. Enjoy these crispy and delicious mushroom risotto balls as a tasty appetiser or snack!

Maple-Glazed Ham with Bourbon and Brown Sugar

Serves: 8

Prep time: 10 minutes / Cook time: 2 hours

Ingredients:
- 1 (2 kg) bone-in ham
- 120ml maple syrup
- 60g brown sugar
- 60ml bourbon
- 1 tablespoon Dijon mustard
- 1 teaspoon ground cloves
- 1/2 teaspoon ground cinnamon
- 1/4 teaspoon ground nutmeg

Preparation instructions:
1. Preheat the Ninja Dual Zone Air Fryer to 160°C on zone 1.
2. Place the ham on the crisper plate of zone 1, and cook for 1 hour.
3. In a small bowl, whisk together the maple syrup, brown sugar, bourbon, Dijon mustard, ground cloves, ground cinnamon, and ground nutmeg until well combined.
4. After 1 hour of cooking, remove the ham from the air fryer, and brush it with half of the glaze.
5. Increase the temperature of zone 1 to 200°C, and return the ham to the air fryer.
6. Cook the ham for another 30 minutes, then brush it with the remaining glaze.
7. Cook for another 30 minutes, or until the internal temperature of the ham reaches 60°C.
8. Remove the ham from the air fryer, and let it rest for 10-15 minutes before slicing and serving.

Turducken Roulade with Cranberry Stuffing

Serves: 10

Prep time: 30 minutes / Cook time: 2 hours

Ingredients:
- For the roulade:
- 1 boneless turkey breast (1.5 kg)
- 1 boneless duck breast (450g)
- 1 boneless chicken breast (450g)
- 1/2 teaspoon garlic powder
- 1/2 teaspoon dried thyme
- 1/2 teaspoon dried oregano
- 1/2 teaspoon salt
- 1/4 teaspoon black pepper
- For the stuffing:
- 240g dried cranberries
- 120ml chicken broth
- 60g chopped fresh parsley
- 60g chopped fresh sage
- 60g chopped fresh thyme
- 60g chopped onion
- 60g chopped celery
- 60g chopped carrot
- 60g butter
- 1/2 teaspoon salt
- 1/4 teaspoon black pepper

Preparation instructions:
1. Preheat the Ninja Dual Zone Air Fryer to 160°C on zone 1.
2. Butterfly the turkey breast and pound it with a meat mallet until it is an even thickness.
3. Season the turkey breast with garlic powder, dried thyme, dried oregano, salt, and black pepper.
4. Layer the duck breast and chicken breast on top of the turkey breast, making sure to

leave a 1-inch border around the edges.

5. To make the stuffing, combine the dried cranberries, chicken broth, chopped fresh parsley, chopped fresh sage, chopped fresh thyme, chopped onion, chopped celery, chopped carrot, butter, salt, and black pepper in a bowl.

6. Spread the stuffing over the chicken breast.

7. Roll the turkey breast around the duck, chicken, and stuffing to form a roulade.

8. Secure the roulade with kitchen twine.

9. Place the roulade on the crisper plate of zone 1, and cook for 1 hour.

10. Increase the temperature of zone 1 to 200°C, and cook for another hour, or until the internal temperature of the roulade reaches 75°C.

11. Remove the roulade from the air fryer, and let it rest for 10-15 minutes before slicing and serving.

Christmas Pudding

Serves: 8

Prep time: 20 minutes / Cook time: 5 hours

Ingredients:

- 225g suet
- 225g sultanas
- 225g raisins
- 225g currants
- 110g candied peel, chopped
- 110g plain flour
- 110g fresh breadcrumbs
- 110g dark brown sugar
- 5g mixed spice
- 2.5g ground cinnamon
- 2.5g freshly grated nutmeg
- 2.5g salt
- 4 medium eggs, beaten
- 150ml stout
- 150ml brown ale

- 50ml brandy
- 50g almonds, blanched and chopped

Preparation instructions:

1. In a large mixing bowl, combine the suet, sultanas, raisins, currants, and candied peel.

2. Add the flour, breadcrumbs, sugar, mixed spice, cinnamon, nutmeg, and salt. Mix well.

3. Add the beaten eggs and mix well.

4. Pour in the stout, brown ale, and brandy, and mix thoroughly.

5. Finally, stir in the chopped almonds.

6. Grease a 1.2-litre pudding basin and spoon the mixture into it. Cover with a double layer of greased greaseproof paper and foil, and secure tightly with string.

7. Place the pudding in the air fryer basket and put it in Zone 1. Set the function to "STEAM" at 100°C for 5 hours.

8. Check the water level every 1-2 hours and top up if necessary.

9. When the cooking time is up, remove the pudding from the air fryer, and let it cool for 10 minutes. Remove the foil and paper, and turn it out onto a plate. Serve warm with brandy butter.

Sweet Potato Casserole with Pecan Streusel Topping

Serves: 6-8

Prep time: 20 minutes / Cook time: 40 minutes

Ingredients:

- 3 medium sweet potatoes, peeled and cubed
- 60g unsalted butter, softened
- 60ml milk
- 60g brown sugar
- 1/2 tsp ground cinnamon
- 1/4 tsp ground nutmeg
- 1/4 tsp salt

- 2 large eggs
- 120g pecans, chopped
- 60g all-purpose flour
- 60g brown sugar
- 2 tbsp unsalted butter, melted
- 1/4 tsp ground cinnamon

Preparation instructions:

1. Preheat your Ninja Dual Zone Air Fryer to 180°C.
2. Boil the sweet potatoes in a large pot of water until tender, about 10-12 minutes. Drain well and transfer to a large mixing bowl.
3. Add the butter, milk, brown sugar, cinnamon, nutmeg, and salt to the mixing bowl. Mash the ingredients together with a potato masher or fork until the mixture is smooth.
4. Beat in the eggs until the mixture is well combined.
5. Transfer the mixture to a greased baking dish and spread it out evenly.
6. In a separate bowl, mix together the pecans, flour, brown sugar, melted butter, and cinnamon to make the streusel topping.
7. Sprinkle the streusel over the sweet potato mixture, spreading it out evenly.
8. Place the baking dish into the air fryer on Zone 1 and select "ROAST" at 180°C for 20 minutes.
9. Once done, remove the dish from the air fryer and allow it to cool for a few minutes before serving.
10. Enjoy your Sweet Potato Casserole with Pecan Streusel Topping as a delicious side dish for your next holiday meal or family gathering!

Balsamic Glazed Roasted Root Vegetables

Serves: 4

Prep time: 10 minutes / Cook time: 25 minutes

Ingredients:

- 500g mixed root vegetables (such as carrots, parsnips, and sweet potatoes), peeled and cut into bite-sized pieces
- 2 tbsp balsamic vinegar
- 1 tbsp honey
- 2 tbsp olive oil
- 2 garlic cloves, minced
- Salt and black pepper, to taste
- Fresh parsley, chopped, for garnish

Preparation instructions:

1. Preheat the Ninja Dual Zone Air Fryer to 200°C on the ROAST setting.
2. In a bowl, whisk together the balsamic vinegar, honey, olive oil, garlic, salt, and pepper.
3. Add the mixed root vegetables to the bowl and toss to coat them evenly with the glaze.
4. Arrange the vegetables on the crisper plate in a single layer, making sure they are not crowded.
5. Select zone 1 and pair it with the ROAST setting at 200°C for 15 minutes.
6. After 15 minutes, remove the crisper plate from zone 1 and toss the vegetables. Place the crisper plate back in zone 1 and roast for another 10 minutes, or until the vegetables are tender and caramelised.
7. Remove from the Ninja Dual Zone Air Fryer and transfer to a serving dish. Garnish with chopped parsley and serve.

Cornish Game Hens with Herb and Citrus Stuffing

Serves: 2

Prep time: 20 minutes / Cook time: 35 minutes

Ingredients:

- 2 Cornish game hens, giblets removed
- 2 slices of bread, diced
- 2 tbsp butter
- 60ml chicken broth
- 60ml orange juice
- 1 tbsp lemon zest
- 1 tbsp fresh thyme, chopped
- 1 tbsp fresh rosemary, chopped
- 1 tbsp fresh parsley, chopped
- Salt and black pepper, to taste
- 2 garlic cloves, minced
- Olive oil, for brushing

Preparation instructions:

1. Preheat the Ninja Dual Zone Air Fryer to 190°C on the ROAST setting.
2. In a skillet over medium heat, melt the butter and sauté the garlic until fragrant. Add the bread cubes and stir until golden brown. Remove from heat and set aside.
3. In a bowl, mix together the chicken broth, orange juice, lemon zest, thyme, rosemary, parsley, salt, and pepper. Add the bread cubes to the bowl and toss to combine.
4. Stuff the Cornish game hens with the herb and citrus stuffing. Brush the hens with olive oil.
5. Place the hens on the crisper plate in zone 2. Select zone 2 and pair it with the ROAST setting at 190°C for 35 minutes.
6. Halfway through the cooking time, flip the hens over and brush with more olive oil. Return to the Ninja Dual Zone Air Fryer to continue cooking until the skin is golden brown and the internal temperature of the hens reaches 74°C.
7. Once done, remove from the Ninja Dual Zone Air Fryer and let rest for 5 minutes. Serve the hens with any remaining stuffing. Enjoy!

Sage and Sausage Stuffing Balls

Serves: 4

Prep time: 20 minutes / Cook time: 25 minutes

Ingredients:

- 450g pork sausage, casings removed
- 1 onion, finely chopped
- 2 garlic cloves, minced
- 2 tbsp butter
- 2 cups cubed bread
- 1 tbsp fresh sage, chopped
- 1 tsp dried thyme
- 1/2 tsp salt
- 1/4 tsp black pepper
- 1 egg, lightly beaten
- 60ml chicken broth

Preparation instructions:

1. Preheat the Ninja Dual Zone Air Fryer to 190°C in zone 2 for 5 minutes.
2. In a skillet, cook the pork sausage, onion, and garlic over medium heat until the sausage is no longer pink. Drain the excess fat.
3. Add the butter, bread cubes, sage, thyme, salt, and pepper. Stir to combine.
4. Remove from heat and let cool for a few minutes.
5. In a separate bowl, whisk together the egg and chicken broth.
6. Add the egg mixture to the skillet and stir to combine.
7. Form the mixture into 12 stuffing balls.
8. Place the stuffing balls in the crisper plate on zone 2 and cook at 190°C for 20-25 minutes,

or until golden brown and crispy on the outside.

Spiced Cranberry Glazed Pork Tenderloin

Serves: 4

Prep time: 10 minutes / Cook time: 25 minutes

Ingredients:

- 1 pork tenderloin (about 450g)
- 1/2 tsp salt
- 1/4 tsp black pepper
- 60ml cranberry sauce
- 1 tbsp honey
- 1 tbsp Dijon mustard
- 1 tsp ground cinnamon
- 1/4 tsp ground ginger
- 1/4 tsp ground cloves

Preparation instructions:

1. Preheat the Ninja Dual Zone Air Fryer to 190°C in zone 2 for 5 minutes.
2. Season the pork tenderloin with salt and black pepper.
3. In a small bowl, whisk together the cranberry sauce, honey, Dijon mustard, cinnamon, ginger, and cloves.
4. Place the pork tenderloin in the crisper plate on zone 2 and cook at 190°C for 10 minutes.
5. Brush the cranberry glaze over the pork tenderloin and continue cooking for an additional 10-15 minutes, or until the internal temperature reaches 63°C.
6. Remove from the air fryer and let rest for a few minutes before slicing and serving.

Eggnog French Toast with Cinnamon Whipped Cream

Serves: 4

Prep time: 10 minutes / Cook time: 20 minutes

Ingredients:
French Toast:
- 4 large eggs
- 240ml of eggnog
- 1 tsp of vanilla extract
- 8 slices of brioche bread
- 2 tbsp of unsalted butter
- 1/4 tsp of ground cinnamon
- 1/8 tsp of ground nutmeg

Cinnamon Whipped Cream:
- 240ml of heavy whipping cream
- 1 tsp of ground cinnamon
- 1 tsp of vanilla extract
- 2 tbsp of granulated sugar

Preparation instructions:

1. In a mixing bowl, whisk together the eggs, eggnog, vanilla extract, cinnamon, and nutmeg until fully combined.
2. Heat the air fryer to 180°C.
3. Dip each slice of brioche bread into the egg mixture, making sure both sides are coated.
4. Melt the butter in a pan or in the microwave.
5. Place the coated bread slices into the air fryer basket and brush with the melted butter.
6. Air fry the French toast for 5 minutes on each side, or until golden brown and crispy.
7. While the French toast is cooking, make the cinnamon whipped cream by whisking together the heavy whipping cream, ground cinnamon, vanilla extract, and granulated sugar until stiff peaks form.
8. Serve the French toast warm, topped with a dollop of cinnamon whipped cream.

Rosemary and Garlic Leg of Lamb with Red Wine Sauce

Serves: 4-6

Prep time: 15 minutes / Cook time: 45 minutes

Ingredients:
* 1 (2kg) leg of lamb
* 3 garlic cloves, minced
* 2 tbsp of fresh rosemary, chopped
* 2 tbsp of olive oil
* Salt and pepper, to taste
* 480ml red wine
* 480ml beef broth
* 2 tbsp of unsalted butter
* 1 tbsp of cornstarch
* 1 tbsp of water

Preparation instructions:
1. Preheat the air fryer to 180°C.
2. In a small mixing bowl, mix together the minced garlic, chopped rosemary, olive oil, salt, and pepper.
3. Rub the mixture all over the leg of lamb.
4. Place the lamb in the air fryer basket and roast for 45 minutes, or until the internal temperature of the lamb reaches 60°C for medium-rare.
5. While the lamb is cooking, make the red wine sauce by combining the red wine and beef broth in a saucepan over medium-high heat.
6. Bring the mixture to a simmer and cook for 10-15 minutes, or until it has reduced by half.
7. In a small bowl, whisk together the cornstarch and water to make a slurry.
8. Add the slurry to the saucepan and whisk to combine.
9. Continue to cook the sauce for 2-3 minutes, or until it has thickened.
10. Remove the saucepan from the heat and whisk in the unsalted butter until fully incorporated.
11. Let the lamb rest for 10 minutes before slicing and serving with the red wine sauce.

Gingerbread Cake with Cream Cheese Frosting

Serves: 8

Prep time: 15 minutes / Cook time: 25 minutes

Ingredients:
For the cake:
* 180g all-purpose flour
* 1 tsp ground ginger
* 1 tsp ground cinnamon
* 1/4 tsp ground cloves
* 1/4 tsp ground nutmeg
* 1 tsp baking powder
* 1/2 tsp baking soda
* 1/4 tsp salt
* 115g unsalted butter, softened
* 100g brown sugar
* 1 large egg
* 120ml molasses
* 120ml hot water
For the frosting:
* 115g cream cheese, softened
* 50g unsalted butter, softened
* 1 tsp vanilla extract
* 125g icing sugar

Preparation instructions:
For the cake:
1. Preheat the Ninja Dual Zone Air Fryer to 160°C.
2. Grease an 8-inch square baking pan.
3. In a medium bowl, whisk together the flour, ginger, cinnamon, cloves, nutmeg, baking powder, baking soda, and salt.
4. In a large bowl, beat the butter and brown

sugar until light and fluffy, about 3 minutes. Add the egg and beat until combined.

5. Beat in the molasses.
6. Gradually beat in the flour mixture until just combined.
7. Add the hot water and stir until smooth.
8. Pour the batter into the prepared pan and smooth the top.
9. Place the pan in zone 1 of the air fryer and bake for 25 minutes, or until a toothpick inserted in the centre comes out clean.
10. Let the cake cool in the pan for 10 minutes before removing it to a wire rack to cool completely.

For the frosting:

1. In a large bowl, beat the cream cheese and butter until smooth.
2. Beat in the vanilla extract.
3. Gradually beat in the icing sugar until the frosting is smooth and creamy.
4. Spread the frosting over the cooled cake.

Candied Yams with Marshmallows and Pecans

Serves: 6

Prep time: 15 minutes / Cook time: 25 minutes

Ingredients:

- 4 medium yams, peeled and cut into 1-inch cubes
- 50g unsalted butter, melted
- 50g brown sugar
- 1/2 tsp ground cinnamon
- 1/4 tsp ground nutmeg
- 1/4 tsp salt
- 50g chopped pecans
- 100g mini marshmallows

Preparation instructions:

1. Preheat the Ninja Dual Zone Air Fryer to 180°C.
2. In a large bowl, toss the yams with the melted butter, brown sugar, cinnamon, nutmeg, and salt.
3. Arrange the yams in a single layer in zone 1 of the air fryer.
4. Cook for 20 minutes, stirring halfway through.
5. In a small bowl, mix together the pecans and marshmallows.
6. Sprinkle the pecan and marshmallow mixture over the yams.
7. Move the yams to zone 2 of the air fryer and cook for an additional 5 minutes, or until the marshmallows are golden brown and toasted.
8. Serve hot and enjoy!

Chapter 8: Snacks and Desserts

Beignets

Serves: 6
Prep time: 20 minutes / Cook time: 8 minutes

Ingredients:

For the dough:
- 250g all-purpose flour
- 2 tsp baking powder
- 1/2 tsp salt
- 1 tbsp granulated sugar
- 120ml milk
- 1 egg, beaten
- 1 tbsp unsalted butter, melted
- Vegetable oil, for frying
- Powdered sugar, for dusting

Preparation instructions:

1. In a large mixing bowl, whisk together flour, baking powder, salt, and sugar.
2. In a separate bowl, combine milk, beaten egg, and melted butter.
3. Gradually pour wet ingredients into the dry mixture and stir to combine. Mix until dough forms a smooth and sticky texture.
4. Cover the bowl with a clean kitchen towel and let it rest for 30 minutes.
5. Preheat the Ninja Dual Zone Air Fryer to 175°C.
6. Pour vegetable oil into the Air Fryer basket and preheat for 2 minutes.
7. Using a small ice cream scoop or spoon, scoop dough into round balls and gently drop into the hot oil.
8. Fry for about 4 minutes or until beignets are golden brown.
9. Use a slotted spoon to remove beignets and place them on a paper towel-lined plate to cool.
10. Dust generously with powdered sugar and serve warm.

Cinnamon Sugar Doughnut Holes

Serves: 6
Prep time: 20 minutes / Cook time: 8 minutes

Ingredients:

For the dough:
- 250g all-purpose flour
- 1 tsp baking powder
- 1/2 tsp salt
- 120g granulated sugar
- 100ml milk
- 1 egg, beaten
- 1 tsp vanilla extract
- 60g unsalted butter, melted
- Vegetable oil, for frying

For the coating:
- 120g granulated sugar
- 1 tsp ground cinnamon

Preparation instructions:

1. In a large mixing bowl, whisk together flour, baking powder, salt, and sugar.
2. In a separate bowl, combine milk, beaten egg, vanilla extract, and melted butter.
3. Gradually pour wet ingredients into the dry mixture and stir to combine. Mix until dough forms a smooth and sticky texture.
4. Cover the bowl with a clean kitchen towel and let it rest for 30 minutes.
5. Preheat the Ninja Dual Zone Air Fryer to 175°C.
6. Pour vegetable oil into the Air Fryer basket and preheat for 2 minutes.
7. Using a small ice cream scoop or spoon, scoop dough into round balls and gently drop into the hot oil.
8. Fry for about 4 minutes or until doughnut holes are golden brown.
9. In a separate bowl, mix sugar and cinnamon together for the coating.

10. Use a slotted spoon to remove doughnut holes and immediately coat them in the cinnamon sugar mixture.
11. Serve warm.

Roasted Beet Chips with Feta Cheese Dip

Serves: 2

Prep time: 10 minutes / Cook time: 20 minutes

Ingredients:

- For the beet chips:
- 2 medium-sized beets
- 1 tbsp olive oil
- Sea salt and black pepper, to taste
- For the feta cheese dip:
- 50g feta cheese
- 2 tbsp Greek yoghurt
- 1 tbsp lemon juice
- 1 tbsp chopped fresh dill
- 1 small garlic clove, minced
- Sea salt and black pepper, to taste

Preparation instructions:

1. Preheat the Ninja Dual Zone Air Fryer to 180°C using the "ROAST" function on zone 2.
2. Wash and peel the beets, and slice them into thin rounds.
3. In a bowl, toss the beet slices with olive oil, salt, and pepper.
4. Arrange the beet slices on the crisper plate on zone 2 of the air fryer, making sure not to overcrowd the plate.
5. Roast the beet slices for 20 minutes, flipping them halfway through the cooking time, until crispy and golden brown.
6. While the beets are roasting, prepare the feta cheese dip by combining all the dip ingredients in a small bowl and mixing until smooth.
7. Serve the beet chips hot with the feta cheese dip on the side.

Salted Caramel Popcorn

Serves: 4

Prep time: 5 minutes / Cook time: 10 minutes

Ingredients:

- 60g popcorn kernels
- 50g unsalted butter
- 50g brown sugar
- 2 tbsp golden syrup
- 1/4 tsp sea salt

Preparation instructions:

1. Preheat the Ninja Dual Zone Air Fryer to 200°C using the "FRY" function on zone 1.
2. Add the popcorn kernels to the crisper basket on zone 1 of the air fryer, making sure they are in a single layer.
3. Fry the popcorn kernels for 10 minutes, shaking the crisper basket occasionally, until all the kernels have popped.
4. While the popcorn is frying, make the salted caramel sauce by melting the butter in a small saucepan over low heat.
5. Add the brown sugar, golden syrup, and salt to the melted butter, and stir until combined.
6. Increase the heat to medium and bring the mixture to a boil, stirring constantly.
7. Remove the saucepan from the heat and pour the salted caramel sauce over the hot popcorn, stirring until all the popcorn is coated.
8. Spread the popcorn in a single layer on a baking sheet and allow it to cool for a few minutes before serving.

S'mores Empanadas with Marshmallow Filling

Serves: 4

Prep time: 20 minutes / Cook time: 10 minutes

Ingredients:

- 1 sheet puff pastry, thawed

- 4 tbsp chocolate chips
- 4 tbsp mini marshmallows
- 1 small egg, beaten
- Graham cracker crumbs, for topping
- Powdered sugar, for dusting

Preparation instructions:

1. Preheat the Ninja Dual Zone Air Fryer to 180°C on "BAKE" function.
2. Cut the puff pastry into 4 squares.
3. Place 1 tablespoon of chocolate chips and 1 tablespoon of mini marshmallows on each square.
4. Fold the puff pastry over the filling to create a triangle shape.
5. Use a fork to press down the edges and seal the empanadas.
6. Brush the empanadas with beaten egg and sprinkle graham cracker crumbs on top.
7. Place the empanadas in the air fryer and bake for 10 minutes or until golden brown.
8. Dust with powdered sugar before serving.

Chocolate and Peanut Butter Stuffed Dates

Serves: 4
Prep time: 10 minutes / Cook time: 5 minutes

Ingredients:

- 8 Medjool dates, pitted
- 4 tsp peanut butter
- 4 tsp chocolate chips
- Sea salt, for topping

Preparation instructions:

1. Preheat the Ninja Dual Zone Air Fryer to 180°C on "ROAST" function.
2. Cut a slit lengthwise on each date and remove the pit.
3. Stuff each date with 1/2 teaspoon of peanut butter and 1/2 teaspoon of chocolate chips.
4. Sprinkle sea salt on top of each date.

5. Place the stuffed dates in the air fryer and roast for 5 minutes or until the chocolate is melted and the dates are slightly caramelised.
6. Serve immediately.

Savory Parmesan Churros with Herb Dip

Serves: 4
Prep time: 15 minutes / Cook time: 12 minutes

Ingredients:

For the churros:
- 150g plain flour
- 1 tsp baking powder
- 1/2 tsp salt
- 1/2 tsp dried oregano
- 1/2 tsp dried basil
- 1/4 tsp garlic powder
- 1/4 tsp onion powder
- 1/8 tsp cayenne pepper
- 120g grated parmesan cheese
- 1 tbsp olive oil
- 240ml boiling water
- Cooking spray

For the herb dip:
- 120g plain Greek yoghurt
- 60g sour cream
- 1 tbsp chopped fresh parsley
- 1 tbsp chopped fresh dill
- 1/4 tsp garlic powder
- Salt and black pepper, to taste

Preparation instructions:

1. Preheat the Ninja Dual Zone Air Fryer to 190°C in zone 1 and 2.
2. In a medium bowl, whisk together the flour, baking powder, salt, oregano, basil, garlic powder, onion powder, cayenne pepper, and parmesan cheese.
3. Add the olive oil and boiling water to the bowl, and stir until a thick dough forms.
4. Fill a pastry bag fitted with a star tip with the

churro dough.

5. Grease the crisper plate with cooking spray.

6. Pipe the churro dough onto the crisper plate, making 10-12 churros.

7. Cook in the air fryer for 10-12 minutes or until golden brown and crisp.

8. While the churros cook, prepare the herb dip. In a small bowl, whisk together the Greek yoghurt, sour cream, parsley, dill, garlic powder, salt, and black pepper.

9. Serve the churros with the herb dip on the side.

Caramelised Banana Bread Pudding

Serves: 4-6
Prep time: 15 minutes / Cook time: 35 minutes

Ingredients:

- 500g cubed day-old bread
- 3 ripe bananas, mashed
- 120g brown sugar
- 2 large eggs
- 1 tsp vanilla extract
- 1/2 tsp ground cinnamon
- 1/4 tsp ground nutmeg
- 1/4 tsp salt
- 480ml whole milk
- For the caramelised bananas:
- 2 ripe bananas, sliced
- 2 tbsp unsalted butter
- 2 tbsp brown sugar

Preparation instructions:

1. Preheat the Ninja Dual Zone Air Fryer to 180°C in zone 1 and 2.

2. Grease a baking dish that fits in the air fryer.

3. In a large bowl, combine the cubed bread, mashed bananas, brown sugar, eggs, vanilla extract, cinnamon, nutmeg, and salt.

4. Pour the whole milk into the bowl, and stir until well combined.

5. Pour the bread mixture into the greased baking dish.

6. Place the baking dish in the air fryer basket and cook for 20-25 minutes or until set and golden brown.

7. While the bread pudding cooks, prepare the caramelised bananas. In a small saucepan, melt the butter and brown sugar over medium heat.

8. Add the sliced bananas to the pan, and cook for 2-3 minutes, stirring occasionally, until caramelised.

9. Serve the bread pudding with the caramelised bananas on top.

Sweet Potato Fries with Cinnamon Sugar and Nutmeg

Serves: 2
Prep time: 10 minutes / Cook time: 22 minutes

Ingredients:

- 450g sweet potatoes, peeled and cut into thin fries
- 1 tbsp olive oil
- 1 tsp ground cinnamon
- 1/2 tsp ground nutmeg
- 2 tbsp granulated sugar
- Salt and black pepper to taste

Preparation instructions:

1. Preheat the Ninja Dual Zone Air Fryer to 200°C.

2. In a mixing bowl, toss the sweet potato fries with olive oil and season with salt and black pepper.

3. Place the sweet potato fries in the air fryer basket and cook in Zone 1 on "AIR FRY" for 12 minutes.

4. In the meantime, mix the cinnamon, nutmeg, and sugar together in a separate bowl.

5. After 12 minutes, transfer the sweet potato fries to Zone 2 and cook on "AIR FRY" for another 10 minutes, until crispy.

6. While the fries are still hot, toss them in the cinnamon sugar mixture and serve immediately.

Lemon-Poppy Seed Scones

Makes: 8 scones

Prep time: 10 minutes / Cook time: 15 minutes

Ingredients:

- 280g plain flour
- 50g caster sugar
- 2 tsp baking powder
- 1/2 tsp baking soda
- 1/2 tsp salt
- 6 tbsp cold unsalted butter, cut into small pieces
- Zest of 2 lemons
- 1 tbsp poppy seeds
- 120ml buttermilk
- 1 large egg
- 1 tsp vanilla extract
- Icing sugar for dusting

Preparation instructions:

1. Preheat the Ninja Dual Zone Air Fryer to 180°C.
2. In a large mixing bowl, whisk together the flour, sugar, baking powder, baking soda, and salt.
3. Add the cold butter to the dry ingredients and use a pastry cutter or your fingertips to cut the butter into the flour mixture until it resembles coarse breadcrumbs.
4. Stir in the lemon zest and poppy seeds.
5. In a separate bowl, whisk together the buttermilk, egg, and vanilla extract.
6. Add the wet ingredients to the dry ingredients and mix until just combined.
7. Turn the dough out onto a floured surface and gently pat it into a circle about 2 cm thick.
8. Use a biscuit cutter to cut out 8 scones and place them on the crisper plate.
9. Bake in Zone 2 on "AIR FRY" for 15 minutes, until the scones are golden brown

and cooked through.

10. Dust with icing sugar and serve warm.

Mini Cherry Pies with Vanilla Bean Ice Cream

Serves: 4

Prep time: 20 minutes / Cook time: 18 minutes

Ingredients:

For the cherry pie filling:
- 400g cherries, pitted and halved
- 2 tbsp cornstarch
- 50g granulated sugar
- 1 tsp lemon juice
- 1/4 tsp ground cinnamon
- 1/4 tsp almond extract

For the pie crust:
- 225g all-purpose flour
- 110g unsalted butter, chilled and cubed
- 1 tbsp granulated sugar
- 1/4 tsp salt
- 4-5 tbsp cold water
- For the vanilla bean ice cream:
- 250ml double cream
- 250ml whole milk
- 5 egg yolks
- 150g granulated sugar
- 1 vanilla bean pod, split and scraped

Preparation instructions:

1. In a medium saucepan, combine the cherries, cornstarch, sugar, lemon juice, cinnamon, and almond extract. Cook over medium heat, stirring occasionally, until the mixture thickens and the cherries are tender. Remove from heat and let cool.
2. To make the pie crust, combine the flour, sugar, and salt in a food processor. Pulse a few times to combine. Add the butter and pulse until the mixture resembles coarse sand. Add the cold water, 1 tablespoon at a time, and pulse until

the dough comes together.

3. Divide the dough into 8 portions and roll each portion into a 4-inch circle. Place 1 tablespoon of the cherry filling in the centre of each circle. Fold the dough over the filling and crimp the edges with a fork.

4. Preheat zone 1 of the Ninja Dual Zone Air Fryer to 200°C on the bake function. Place the pies on the crisper plate and bake for 8-10 minutes, or until golden brown.

5. To make the vanilla bean ice cream, combine the cream and milk in a medium saucepan. Heat over medium heat until steaming.

6. In a separate bowl, whisk together the egg yolks and sugar until pale and fluffy. Slowly pour the hot milk mixture into the egg mixture, whisking constantly. Return the mixture to the saucepan and cook over low heat, stirring constantly, until thick enough to coat the back of a spoon.

7. Remove from heat and stir in the vanilla bean seeds. Strain the mixture through a fine-mesh sieve and let cool. Churn the mixture in an ice cream maker according to the manufacturer's instructions.

8. Serve the warm cherry pies with a scoop of vanilla bean ice cream.

Cinnamon and Sugar Fried Wontons with Vanilla Cream Dip

Serves: 4

Prep time: 15 minutes / Cook time: 10 minutes

Ingredients:
For the wontons:
- 16 wonton wrappers
- 60g granulated sugar
- 1 tsp ground cinnamon
- Vegetable oil, for frying

For the vanilla cream dip:
- 120ml double cream
- 60g icing sugar
- 1/4 tsp vanilla extract

Preparation instructions:
1. In a small bowl, combine the granulated sugar, cinnamon, and nutmeg.
2. Lay out the wonton wrappers on a clean surface.
3. Sprinkle the cinnamon sugar mixture evenly over each wonton wrapper.
4. Fold each wonton in half diagonally to form a triangle and press the edges together to seal.
5. Heat the Ninja Dual Zone Air Fryer on Zone 1 at 200°C for 3 minutes.
6. Brush the wontons with vegetable oil on both sides.
7. Place the wontons in the air fryer basket in a single layer and cook on Zone 1 at 200°C for 5-6 minutes or until golden brown and crispy.
8. While the wontons are cooking, make the vanilla cream dip. In a medium bowl, whisk together the heavy cream, powdered sugar, and vanilla extract until stiff peaks form.
9. Once the wontons are done cooking, remove them from the air fryer basket and transfer to a plate.
10. Serve the cinnamon and sugar fried wontons warm with the vanilla cream dip on the side.
11. Enjoy your delicious and easy-to-make Cinnamon and Sugar Fried Wontons with Vanilla Cream Dip, made in your Ninja Dual Zone Air Fryer!

Chocolate Lava Cakes with Raspberry Coulis

Serves: 4

Prep time: 15 minutes / Cook time: 10 minutes

Ingredients:
- For the cakes:
- 110g dark chocolate, chopped
- 110g unsalted butter, cubed

- 60g caster sugar
- 2 large eggs
- 2 egg yolks
- 40g plain flour
- 1 tsp vanilla extract
- For the raspberry coulis:
- 150g raspberries
- 1 tbsp icing sugar
- 1 tsp lemon juice

Preparation instructions:

1. Preheat the Ninja Dual Zone Air Fryer on Zone 1 at 180°C for 5 minutes.
2. Grease four ramekins with butter and dust with cocoa powder.
3. Melt the chocolate and butter in a heatproof bowl over a pot of simmering water.
4. In a separate bowl, whisk together the sugar, eggs, egg yolks, and vanilla extract until pale and frothy.
5. Fold in the melted chocolate and butter, then fold in the flour until just combined.
6. Pour the batter into the prepared ramekins, filling each one two-thirds of the way full.
7. Place the ramekins in Zone 1 of the air fryer and select "BAKE" for 10 minutes.
8. While the cakes are baking, make the raspberry coulis. In a blender, combine the raspberries, icing sugar, and lemon juice until smooth.
9. Once the cakes are done, carefully remove them from the air fryer and let them cool for a few minutes.
10. To serve, carefully invert each cake onto a plate and drizzle with the raspberry coulis.

Caramelized Onion and Gruyere Tartlets

Serves: 6

Prep time: 20 minutes / Cook time: 20 minutes

Ingredients:

For the pastry:
- 175g plain flour
- 85g unsalted butter, chilled and cubed
- 1 egg yolk
- 2-3 tbsp cold water

For the filling:
- 1 tbsp olive oil
- 2 large onions, thinly sliced
- 1 tbsp balsamic vinegar
- 1 tsp caster sugar
- 1/2 tsp dried thyme
- 100g Gruyere cheese, grated
- 2 large eggs
- 150ml double cream
- Salt and black pepper, to taste

Preparation instructions:

1. Preheat the Ninja Dual Zone Air Fryer on Zone 1 at 180°C for 5 minutes.
2. To make the pastry, pulse the flour and butter in a food processor until the mixture resembles breadcrumbs. Add the egg yolk and water and pulse until the dough comes together.
3. Roll out the pastry on a floured surface and use it to line six tartlet tins.
4. Use a fork to prick holes in the centre of each square, leaving a 1cm border around the edges.
5. Heat the olive oil in a skillet over medium heat. Add the sliced onions and cook until they are soft and caramelised, about 15-20 minutes.
6. Add the balsamic vinegar, brown sugar, thyme, salt, and pepper to the skillet. Stir and cook for an additional 5 minutes.
7. Spoon the onion mixture onto each puff pastry square, leaving a 1cm border around the edges. Brush the beaten egg onto the edges of the puff pastry.
8. Sprinkle the grated Gruyere cheese over the onion mixture.
9. Place the tartlets onto the crisper plate and select zone 1. Roast the tartlets for 12-15

minutes until the pastry is golden brown and puffed up.

10. Serve hot or at room temperature.

Churro Bites with Dulce de Leche Dip

Serves: 4

Prep time: 15 minutes / Cook time: 10 minutes

Ingredients:

- For the churros:
- 60g unsalted butter
- 1/4 tsp salt
- 1 tsp granulated sugar
- 120ml water
- 75g plain flour
- 1 large egg
- 1/4 tsp vanilla extract
- 1/2 tsp ground cinnamon
- 60g granulated sugar
- 1/4 tsp ground cinnamon
- 2 tsp vegetable oil
- For the dip:
- 120g dulce de leche
- 60ml double cream

Preparation instructions:

1. Preheat the Ninja Dual Zone Air Fryer to 180°C using the "AIR FRY" function.
2. In a medium saucepan, combine butter, salt, sugar, and water over medium heat. Bring to a boil, stirring occasionally.
3. Reduce heat to low and add flour, stirring constantly with a wooden spoon until the mixture forms a smooth ball. Remove from heat.
4. Add egg, vanilla extract, and cinnamon to the mixture, stirring until smooth.
5. Transfer the mixture to a piping bag fitted with a star nozzle.
6. Pipe small rounds of dough into the air fryer

basket. Lightly brush each churro with vegetable oil.

7. Cook for 10 minutes or until golden brown and crispy.
8. In a small bowl, combine the sugar and cinnamon. Roll the hot churros in the mixture until coated.
9. For the dip, combine the dulce de leche and double cream in a microwave-safe bowl. Microwave for 30 seconds, then stir until smooth.
10. Serve the churros warm with the dulce de leche dip on the side.

Cheesy Broccoli Bites

Serves: 4

Prep time: 15 minutes / Cook time: 12 minutes

Ingredients:

- 250g broccoli, finely chopped
- 120g cheddar cheese, grated
- 120g plain breadcrumbs
- 60g grated parmesan cheese
- 1 large egg, beaten
- 1 garlic clove, minced
- 1/4 tsp salt
- 1/4 tsp black pepper
- 2 tsp olive oil

Preparation instructions:

1. Preheat the Ninja Dual Zone Air Fryer to 200°C using the "AIR FRY" function.
2. In a large bowl, mix together the broccoli, cheddar cheese, breadcrumbs, parmesan cheese, egg, garlic, salt, and pepper.
3. Form the mixture into small, bite-sized balls.
4. Brush the air fryer basket with olive oil.
5. Arrange the broccoli bites in a single layer in the basket.
6. Air fry for 12 minutes or until golden brown and crispy.
7. Serve hot with your favourite dipping sauce.

Chapter 9: Staples, Sauces, Dips, and Dressings

Baked Garlic and Herb Croutons

Serves: 4

Prep time: 10 minutes / Cook time: 15 minutes

Ingredients:

- 4 slices of bread (white, brown, or sourdough)
- 2 cloves of garlic, finely minced
- 2 tbsp olive oil
- 1 tbsp dried mixed herbs (such as oregano, thyme, and rosemary)
- Salt and black pepper to taste

Preparation instructions:

1. Preheat the Ninja Dual Zone Air Fryer to 180°C on "BAKE" function.
2. Cut the bread slices into small cubes and place them in a bowl.
3. Add the minced garlic, olive oil, dried mixed herbs, salt, and black pepper to the bowl. Toss until the bread cubes are well coated.
4. Place the seasoned bread cubes in the crisper basket of the Ninja Dual Zone Air Fryer.
5. Select zone 1 and pair it with "BAKE" at 180°C for 10 minutes. Select zone 2 and pair it with "BAKE" at 180°C for 15 minutes. Select "SYNC" followed by the "START/STOP" button.
6. Halfway through cooking, shake the basket to ensure the croutons are evenly cooked.
7. Once cooked, remove the croutons from the air fryer and allow them to cool before serving.

Caramelized Watermelon Cubes

Serves: 4

Prep time: 5 minutes / Cook time: 10 minutes

Ingredients:

- 1 small seedless watermelon, cut into 1-inch cubes
- 1 tbsp honey
- 1 tbsp balsamic vinegar
- Pinch of salt

Preparation instructions:

1. Preheat the Ninja Dual Zone Air Fryer to 200°C on "AIR FRY" function.
2. In a small bowl, mix together the honey, balsamic vinegar, and salt.
3. Place the watermelon cubes in the crisper basket of the air fryer.
4. Brush the honey mixture over the watermelon cubes.
5. Select zone 1 and pair it with "AIR FRY" at 200°C for 5 minutes. Select zone 2 and pair it with "AIR FRY" at 200°C for 10 minutes. Select "SYNC" followed by the "START/STOP" button.
6. Halfway through cooking, turn the watermelon cubes over and brush the other side with the remaining honey mixture.
7. Once cooked, remove the watermelon cubes from the air fryer and allow them to cool for a few minutes before serving.

Roasted Garlic Hummus

Serves: 4-6

Prep time: 10 minutes / Cook time: 40 minutes

Ingredients:

- 1 can (400g) chickpeas, drained and rinsed
- 1 head of garlic
- 2 tbsp tahini
- 3 tbsp extra-virgin olive oil
- 2 tbsp lemon juice
- 1/2 tsp salt
- 1/4 tsp ground cumin
- 2-3 tbsp water

- Paprika and olive oil, for garnish

Preparation instructions:

1. Preheat the Ninja Dual Zone Air Fryer to 200°C on the roast setting.
2. Cut off the top of the garlic head to expose the cloves. Place the garlic on a sheet of aluminium foil and drizzle with 1 tbsp of olive oil.
3. Wrap the foil tightly around the garlic and place it in the Ninja Dual Zone Air Fryer. Roast for 40 minutes until the garlic is soft and fragrant.
4. Remove the garlic from the air fryer and allow it to cool slightly.
5. In a food processor, combine the chickpeas, tahini, remaining olive oil, lemon juice, salt, and cumin.
6. Squeeze the roasted garlic cloves out of their skins and add them to the food processor.
7. Process the mixture until it is smooth and creamy. If the mixture is too thick, add 2-3 tbsp of water until it reaches your desired consistency.
8. Taste and adjust seasoning if necessary.
9. Transfer the hummus to a serving bowl and garnish with a drizzle of olive oil and a sprinkle of paprika. Serve with pita bread or vegetables for dipping.

Jalapeño-Cilantro Hummus

Serves: 4-6

Prep time: 10 minutes / Cook time: 5 minutes

Ingredients:

- 1 can (400g) chickpeas, drained and rinsed
- 1 jalapeño pepper, seeded and roughly chopped
- 120g fresh cilantro leaves
- 2 tbsp tahini
- 2 tbsp extra-virgin olive oil
- 2 tbsp lemon juice
- 1/2 tsp salt
- 1/4 tsp ground cumin
- 2-3 tbsp water

Preparation instructions:

1. In a food processor, combine the chickpeas, jalapeño pepper, cilantro, tahini, olive oil, lemon juice, salt, and cumin.
2. Process the mixture until it is smooth and creamy. If the mixture is too thick, add 2-3 tbsp of water until it reaches your desired consistency.
3. Taste and adjust seasoning if necessary.
4. Add the mixture to the air fryer basket and air fry at 160°C for 5 minutes.
5. Transfer the hummus to a serving bowl and serve with pita bread or vegetables for dipping.
6. Note: For a spicier hummus, leave the seeds in the jalapeño pepper. For a milder hummus, remove the seeds and membrane.

Sun-Dried Tomato Tapenade

Serves: 4

Prep time: 10 minutes / Cook time: 5 minutes

Ingredients:

- 240g sun-dried tomatoes, packed in oil
- 60g pitted kalamata olives
- 60g fresh basil leaves
- 2 cloves garlic, peeled
- 2 tbsp capers
- 2 tbsp olive oil
- 2 tbsp freshly squeezed lemon juice
- Salt and black pepper to taste

Preparation instructions:

1. Drain the sun-dried tomatoes from the oil and roughly chop them.
2. Add the sun-dried tomatoes, kalamata olives, basil leaves, garlic, capers, olive oil, and lemon juice to a food processor. Pulse until a coarse paste forms.
3. Season with salt and black pepper to taste.
4. Add the mixture to the air fryer basket and air fry at 160°C for 5 minutes.

5. Serve the tapenade with bread, crackers, or vegetable sticks.

Crispy Tofu Bites

Serves: 2

Prep time: 10 minutes / Cook time: 20 minutes

Ingredients:
- 1 block (400g) firm tofu
- 2 tbsp cornstarch
- 2 tbsp soy sauce
- 1 tbsp rice vinegar
- 1 tsp garlic powder
- 1/2 tsp ground ginger
- 1/4 tsp cayenne pepper
- 120g panko breadcrumbs
- Salt and black pepper to taste
- Cooking spray

Preparation instructions:
1. Preheat the Ninja Dual Zone Air Fryer to 200°C on Air Fry mode.
2. Drain the tofu and cut it into small bite-sized cubes.
3. In a shallow bowl, whisk together the cornstarch, soy sauce, rice vinegar, garlic powder, ginger, and cayenne pepper.
4. In another shallow bowl, mix the panko breadcrumbs with salt and black pepper to taste.
5. Dip each tofu cube into the cornstarch mixture, shaking off any excess, and then roll it in the panko mixture, pressing to coat.
6. Place the coated tofu cubes in the crisper plate and spray with cooking spray.
7. Select zone 1 and pair it with "AIR FRY" at 200°C for 10 minutes. Select zone 2 and pair it with "AIR FRY" at 200°C for 20 minutes. Select "SYNC" followed by the "START/ STOP" button.
8. Halfway through cooking, shake the crisper

plate to ensure even cooking.
9. Once done, remove the tofu bites from the air fryer and serve hot with your favourite dipping sauce.

Baked Zucchini Blooms

Serves: 4

Prep time: 15 minutes / Cook time: 10 minutes

Ingredients:
- 8-10 zucchini blooms
- 120g ricotta cheese
- 1 tablespoon chopped fresh basil
- 1 tablespoon chopped fresh parsley
- 1 small garlic clove, minced
- 2 tablespoons grated parmesan cheese
- 120g all-purpose flour
- 1 egg
- 120g panko breadcrumbs
- Salt and pepper to taste
- Cooking spray

Preparation instructions:
1. Preheat the Ninja Dual Zone Air Fryer to 190°C on "BAKE" mode.
2. In a small bowl, mix the ricotta cheese, basil, parsley, garlic, and parmesan cheese until well combined.
3. Carefully remove the stamen from each zucchini bloom and gently rinse the blooms under cold running water. Pat dry with paper towels.
4. Stuff each zucchini bloom with about 1 tablespoon of the ricotta mixture and twist the ends of the petals to seal.
5. Place the flour in a shallow dish. In another shallow dish, whisk the egg. In a third shallow dish, combine the panko breadcrumbs with salt and pepper.
6. Dredge each stuffed zucchini bloom in the flour, shaking off any excess. Then dip it in the egg, followed by the breadcrumb

mixture, pressing gently to coat.

7. Place the breaded zucchini blooms in the air fryer basket, making sure they do not touch each other. Spray the tops lightly with cooking spray.

8. Air fry for 8-10 minutes or until the blooms are crispy and golden brown.

9. Remove from the air fryer and serve immediately with your favourite dipping sauce.

Fruit Leathers

Serves: 6-8

Prep time: 10 minutes / Cook time: 3-4 hours

Ingredients:

- 800g fresh fruit (such as strawberries, blueberries, peaches, or mangoes)
- 1 tablespoon honey
- 1 tablespoon lemon juice

Preparation instructions:

1. Preheat the Ninja Dual Zone Air Fryer to 65°C in DEHYDRATE mode.

2. Line the dehydration trays with parchment paper.

3. Wash and chop the fruit into small pieces, discarding any pits or tough stems.

4. In a blender, puree the fruit with honey and lemon juice until smooth.

5. Pour the fruit puree onto the parchment paper-lined dehydration trays, spreading it evenly with a spatula.

6. Place the trays in the air fryer and set the timer for 3-4 hours.

7. After 2 hours, check the fruit leather and rotate the trays if necessary.

8. Continue to check the fruit leather every 30 minutes until it is dry and slightly tacky to the touch.

9. Once the fruit leather is dry, remove it from the air fryer and let it cool completely.

10. Peel the fruit leather off the parchment paper and cut it into strips with a pair of scissors.

11. Roll up the strips and store them in an airtight container for up to a month.

Mushroom Jerky

Serves: 4

Prep time: 10 minutes / Dehydrate time: 6 hours

Ingredients:

- 450g mushrooms, sliced (white button, shiitake or portobello)
- 2 tbsp soy sauce
- 1 tbsp Worcestershire sauce
- 1 tbsp liquid smoke
- 1 tsp smoked paprika
- 1 tsp garlic powder
- 1 tsp onion powder
- 1/2 tsp black pepper

Preparation instructions:

1. Preheat the Ninja Dual Zone Air Fryer to 70°C using the dehydrate function.

2. In a mixing bowl, combine soy sauce, Worcestershire sauce, liquid smoke, smoked paprika, garlic powder, onion powder, and black pepper. Mix well.

3. Add the sliced mushrooms into the bowl with the sauce mixture. Mix well, ensuring that each mushroom is evenly coated.

4. Place the mushrooms on the dehydrate rack in a single layer. Place the rack in zone 1 of the Ninja Dual Zone Air Fryer.

5. Set the dehydrate function to 6 hours and start the air fryer. Check the mushrooms halfway through the cooking time, and flip them over to ensure even dehydration.

6. Once done, remove the mushrooms from the dehydrate rack and store in an airtight container.

Spaghetti Nests

Serves: 4

Prep time: 10 minutes / Cook time: 10 minutes

Ingredients:
- 250g spaghetti
- 1 egg
- 60g grated Parmesan cheese
- 2 tbsp chopped fresh parsley
- Salt and pepper
- 1 tbsp olive oil

Preparation instructions:
1. Preheat the Ninja Dual Zone Air Fryer to 180°C using the air fry function.
2. Cook spaghetti according to package instructions. Once cooked, drain and rinse under cold water.
3. In a mixing bowl, whisk the egg and add Parmesan cheese, parsley, salt and pepper. Mix well.
4. Add the cooked spaghetti to the egg mixture and toss until the spaghetti is coated evenly.
5. Grease the air fryer basket with olive oil. Use a fork to twirl the spaghetti into a nest shape and place it into the air fryer basket.
6. Place the basket in zone 2 of the Ninja Dual Zone Air Fryer and air fry for 10 minutes, or until the spaghetti nests are crispy and golden.
7. Remove from the air fryer and serve immediately. Optional: garnish with additional Parmesan cheese and parsley.

Stuffed Mushrooms with Sausage and Cheese

Serves: 4

Prep time: 20 minutes / Cook time: 20 minutes

Ingredients:
- 8 large button mushrooms
- 500g ground sausage
- 120g shredded mozzarella cheese
- 60g chopped onion
- 60g chopped green bell pepper
- 60g chopped red bell pepper
- 60g chopped celery
- 1/2 teaspoon garlic powder
- 1/2 teaspoon dried oregano
- 1/4 teaspoon salt
- 1/4 teaspoon black pepper
- 1 tablespoon olive oil

Preparation instructions:
1. Preheat the Ninja Dual Zone Air Fryer to 180°C in zone 1, using the "ROAST" function.
2. Remove the stems from the mushrooms and chop them finely.
3. In a skillet over medium heat, cook the sausage until browned, stirring frequently.
4. Add the chopped mushroom stems, onion, green and red bell peppers, celery, garlic powder, oregano, salt, and pepper. Cook until vegetables are tender, stirring occasionally.
5. Place the mushroom caps on a baking sheet and brush them with olive oil.
6. Spoon the sausage mixture into each mushroom cap and top with shredded mozzarella cheese.
7. Place the stuffed mushrooms in zone 2 of the air fryer and select the "AIR FRY" function at 180°C for 10 minutes.
8. Serve hot.

Baked Ziti with Tomato Sauce and Mozzarella Cheese

Serves: 6

Prep time: 20 minutes / Cook time: 30 minutes

Ingredients:
- 500g ziti pasta
- 1 jar (680g) tomato sauce
- 120g grated Parmesan cheese
- 120g shredded mozzarella cheese
- 120g chopped fresh basil
- 1/2 teaspoon salt
- 1/2 teaspoon black pepper

- 1/2 teaspoon dried oregano
- 1/2 teaspoon garlic powder

Preparation instructions:
1. Preheat the Ninja Dual Zone Air Fryer to 180°C in zone 1, using the "BAKE" function.
2. Cook the ziti pasta according to the package instructions until al dente, and then drain.
3. In a large bowl, mix the cooked pasta with tomato sauce, Parmesan cheese, shredded mozzarella cheese, fresh basil, salt, black pepper, oregano, and garlic powder.
4. Pour the pasta mixture into a baking dish that fits in zone 2 of the air fryer.
5. Cover the baking dish with foil and place it in zone 2.
6. Select the "BAKE" function at 180°C for 20 minutes.
7. Remove the foil from the baking dish and continue baking for another 10 minutes until the cheese is melted and bubbly.
8. Serve hot.

Stuffed Peppers with Rice and Ground Beef

Serves: 4

Prep time: 20 minutes / Cook time: 30 minutes

Ingredients:
For the stuffed peppers:
- 4 large bell peppers, cut the top off and remove the seeds
- 500g ground beef
- 120g cooked rice
- 60g chopped onion
- 60g chopped celery
- 60g chopped carrots
- 1 garlic clove, minced
- 1 teaspoon dried oregano
- Salt and pepper to taste
- 120g shredded cheddar cheese

For the tomato sauce:
- 1 can (14.5 oz) crushed tomatoes

- 1 garlic clove, minced
- 1 teaspoon dried basil
- Salt and pepper to taste

Preparation instructions:
1. Preheat the Ninja Dual Zone Air Fryer to 375°F using the "Bake" function on both zones.
2. In a large bowl, combine ground beef, cooked rice, onion, celery, carrots, garlic, oregano, salt, and pepper. Mix well.
3. Stuff each pepper with the beef and rice mixture. Place the stuffed peppers in the air fryer basket of zone 1.
4. In a small bowl, combine the crushed tomatoes, garlic, basil, salt, and pepper to make the tomato sauce. Pour the sauce over the stuffed peppers.
5. Sprinkle shredded cheddar cheese on top of each pepper.
6. Place the air fryer basket in zone 1 and bake for 30 minutes.
7. Once the peppers are cooked, remove from the air fryer and let them cool for a few minutes before serving.

Jalapeno Poppers with Spicy Mayo Dip

Serves: 4

Prep time: 15 minutes / Cook time: 10 minutes

Ingredients:
For the jalapeno poppers:
- 8 jalapeno peppers, sliced in half lengthwise, seeds and membranes removed
- 113g cream cheese, softened
- 120g shredded cheddar cheese
- 1/4 teaspoon garlic powder
- Salt and pepper to taste
- 120g panko breadcrumbs
- 1 large egg, beaten

For the spicy mayo dip:
- 120g mayonnaise
- 1 tablespoon sriracha sauce

- 1/2 tablespoon lemon juice
- Salt and pepper to taste

Preparation instructions:

1. Preheat the Ninja Dual Zone Air Fryer to 400°F using the "Air Fry" function on zone 1.
2. In a medium bowl, combine cream cheese, cheddar cheese, garlic powder, salt, and pepper. Mix well.
3. Stuff each jalapeno half with the cream cheese mixture.
4. In a shallow dish, beat the egg. In another shallow dish, place the panko breadcrumbs.
5. Dip each stuffed jalapeno half in the beaten egg, and then coat it with the panko breadcrumbs.
6. Place the coated jalapeno halves in the air fryer basket of zone 1.
7. Air fry for 10 minutes, or until the jalapenos are golden brown and crispy.
8. In a small bowl, combine mayonnaise, sriracha sauce, lemon juice, salt, and pepper to make the spicy mayo dip.
9. Serve the jalapeno poppers hot with the spicy mayo dip on the side. Enjoy!

Corn on the Cob with Herb Butter

Serves: 4

Prep time: 5 minutes / Cook time: 12 minutes

Ingredients:

- 4 corn on the cob, husks removed
- 4 tbsp unsalted butter, at room temperature
- 2 tbsp chopped fresh parsley
- 2 tbsp chopped fresh chives
- 1 garlic clove, minced
- Salt and black pepper, to taste

Preparation instructions:

1. Preheat the Ninja Dual Zone Air Fryer to 200°C on roast setting.
2. In a small bowl, mix the butter, parsley, chives, and garlic until well combined.
3. Season the corn with salt and pepper, and then, spread the herb butter over each corn cob.

4. Place the corn on the cob in the air fryer basket of Zone 2.
5. Roast the corn on the cob for 12 minutes or until the corn is cooked and lightly browned.
6. Serve hot and enjoy!

Buffalo Cauliflower Bites with Blue Cheese Dip

Serves: 4

Prep time: 10 minutes / Cook time: 20 minutes

Ingredients:

- 1 head cauliflower, cut into small florets
- 50g plain flour
- 50ml milk
- 1 tsp garlic powder
- 1 tsp onion powder
- 1 tsp paprika
- 1/2 tsp salt
- 1/2 tsp black pepper
- 60ml buffalo sauce
- 1 tbsp unsalted butter, melted

For the blue cheese dip:

- 100g sour cream
- 50g crumbled blue cheese
- 1 tbsp lemon juice
- Salt and black pepper, to taste

Preparation instructions:

1. Preheat the Ninja Dual Zone Air Fryer to 200°C on fry setting.
2. In a large bowl, whisk together the flour, milk, garlic powder, onion powder, paprika, salt, and black pepper until smooth.
3. Dip each cauliflower floret in the batter, shake off any excess, and place them in the air fryer basket of Zone 1.
4. Fry the cauliflower florets for 10 minutes, shaking the basket halfway through cooking.
5. Meanwhile, in a small bowl, mix the buffalo sauce and melted butter.
6. After 10 minutes, remove the basket from the air fryer and toss the cauliflower florets with the buffalo sauce mixture.

7. Return the basket to the air fryer and fry for an additional 10 minutes.
8. In the meantime, make the blue cheese dip: In a small bowl, mix together the sour cream, blue cheese, lemon juice, salt, and black pepper until well combined.
9. Serve the buffalo cauliflower bites hot with the blue cheese dip on the side. Enjoy!

Pita Chips with Za'atar and Olive Oil

Serves: 4

Prep time: 5 minutes / Cook time: 8 minutes

Ingredients:
- 4 pita breads, cut into small triangles
- 2 tbsp olive oil
- 2 tbsp za'atar seasoning
- Salt and black pepper, to taste

Preparation instructions:
1. Preheat the Ninja Dual Zone Air Fryer by selecting "ZONE 1" and "AIR FRY" at 200°C for 3 minutes.
2. In a mixing bowl, toss the pita triangles with olive oil, za'atar seasoning, salt, and pepper until coated evenly.
3. Remove the crisper plate from Zone 1, and spread the pita triangles on it in a single layer.
4. Place the crisper plate in Zone 1 and select "AIR FRY" at 200°C for 8 minutes.
5. When done, remove the crisper plate from the air fryer, let the pita chips cool for a minute or two, and serve.

Cinnamon Sugar Pretzel Bites with Cream Cheese Dip

Serves: 4

Prep time: 15 minutes / Cook time: 12 minutes

Ingredients:
For the pretzel bites:
- 360g all-purpose flour
- 1 tbsp granulated sugar
- 1/2 tsp salt
- 1/2 tsp instant yeast
- 120ml warm water
- 1 tbsp unsalted butter, melted
- 60g baking soda
- 700ml hot water
- 60g unsalted butter, melted
- 60g granulated sugar
- 1 tsp ground cinnamon

For the cream cheese dip:
- 113g cream cheese, softened
- 60g powdered sugar
- 1/4 tsp vanilla extract

Preparation instructions:
For the pretzel bites:
1. In a mixing bowl, whisk together flour, sugar, salt, and instant yeast. Add warm water and melted butter, and mix until the dough forms a ball.
2. Knead the dough on a floured surface for 5 minutes, until it becomes smooth and elastic.
3. Cover the dough with a clean towel and let it rise for 10 minutes.
4. Meanwhile, in a mixing bowl, dissolve baking soda in hot water and set aside.
5. Preheat the Ninja Dual Zone Air Fryer by selecting "ZONE 1" and "AIR FRY" at 200°C for 3 minutes.
6. Divide the dough into small balls, about 1 inch in diameter.
7. Dip each ball into the baking soda solution for a few seconds, and then place them on the crisper plate in Zone 1.
8. Brush melted butter over each ball, and then sprinkle cinnamon sugar on top.
9. Air fry the pretzel bites in Zone 1 for 12 minutes at 200°C.

For the cream cheese dip:
1. In a mixing bowl, beat softened cream cheese until smooth.
2. Add powdered sugar and vanilla extract, and beat until well combined.
3. Serve the pretzel bites with the cream cheese dip on the side.

Mini Sticky Toffee Puddings

Servings: 4

Prep Time: 5 minutes / Cook Time: 10 minutes

Ingredients

- 4 large chocolate chip muffins
- 50g large raisins
- 1cal butter fry spray

For the sauce
- 25g light muscovado sugar
- 25g dark muscovado sugar
- 50g butter
- 75ml heavy cream
- 200g vanilla ice cream

Preparation instructions:

1. Hand crumbled the muffins and combine them with the raisins
2. Place these ingredients into a 4 greased mini baking pots
3. Cover the baking dish with foil and place 2 in each zone draw
4. Select the zones, using the 'BAKE' function at 200°C for 9 minutes
5. Press 'MATCH' and then 'START/STOP' to bake
6. In the meantime, amalgamate the muscovado sugar variants with the butter and cream, followed by heating them in a small fry pan
7. Continue stirring the mixture until the sugar caramelised and forms toffee sauce
8. Retrieve the muffin based mixture from the ninja foodi duel zone and cover with the toffee sauce
9. Dollop 50g of vanilla ice-cream onto each pot.

Brownie Bites with Peanut Butter Frosting

Servings: 16 bites

Prep Time: 10 minutes / Cook Time: 8 minutes

Ingredients:
For the brownies:
- 136 grams all-purpose flour
- 100 grams unsweetened cocoa powder
- 1 teaspoon baking powder
- 1/2 teaspoon salt
- 113 grams unsalted butter, melted
- 201 grams granulated sugar
- 2 large eggs
- 1 teaspoon vanilla extract

For the frosting:
- 113 grams creamy peanut butter
- 57 grams unsalted butter, at room temperature
- 402 grams powdered sugar
- 2-3 tablespoons milk

Preparation instructions:

1. To make the brownies, combine the flour, cocoa powder, baking powder, and salt in a large bowl.
2. In a separate bowl, beat together the melted butter, sugar, eggs, and vanilla extract. Add the dry ingredients, and stir until just combined.
3. Using a cookie scoop or a tablespoon, drop the batter into 16 portions in the air fryer basket.
4. Air fry at 350°F for 6-8 minutes, or until a toothpick inserted into the center of a brownie bite comes out clean.
5. To make the frosting, beat together the peanut butter and butter in a large bowl until

creamy. Gradually add the powdered sugar, and continue to beat until well combined. Gradually add the milk, 1 tablespoon at a time, until the frosting reaches the desired consistency.

6. Once the brownie bites have cooled, spread or pipe the frosting onto each one.

7. Serve and enjoy!

Peach Cobbler

Servings: 4

Prep Time: 15 minutes / Cook Time: 15 minutes (plus time to come to pressure and release pressure)

Ingredients:

- 68 grams all-purpose flour
- 100 grams granulated sugar
- 1/2 tsp baking powder
- 1/4 tsp salt
- 118 ml milk
- 57 grams unsalted butter, melted
- 1 tsp vanilla extract
- 256 grams sliced peaches (fresh or frozen)
- 57 grams brown sugar
- 1 tsp ground cinnamon
- 60 ml water

Preparation instructions:

1. The flour, sugar, baking powder, and salt should all be combined in a medium bowl and whisked together.

2. Add the milk, melted butter, and vanilla extract and stir until just combined.

3. In a separate bowl, toss together the sliced peaches, brown sugar, and cinnamon.

4. Lightly grease a pressure cooker-friendly baking dish, about 6 inches in diameter. Pour the peach mixture into the dish and spread it evenly.

5. Pour the batter over the top of the peaches, but do not stir.

6. Pour the water over the batter.

7. Cover the baking dish with foil and place it on the trivet inside the pressure cooker. Add 250 ml of water to the pressure cooker.

8. Close the lid and set the pressure cooker to cook on high pressure for 15 minutes.

9. After 15 minutes, let the pressure release naturally for 10 minutes, then manually release any remaining pressure.

10. Carefully remove the baking dish from the pressure cooker using oven mitts. Remove the foil and let the cobbler cool for a few minutes before serving.

11. Serve the cobbler warm, with a scoop of vanilla ice cream on top, if desired.

Mixed Berry Cupcakes

Serves 8

Prep time: 10 minutes / Cook time: 15 minutes

Ingredients

- 200g self-raising flour
- A pinch of kosher salt
- 1 tsp vanilla bean paste
- 1 tsp ground cinnamon
- 2 medium eggs, beaten
- 200g mixed berries, fresh or frozen
- 150g brown sugar
- 100g butter, melted

Buttercream:

- 600g icing sugar
- 300g butter, room temperature
- 1 tsp vanilla bean extract

Preparation instructions

1. Remove a crisper plate from your Nina Foodi. Preheat the Ninja Foodi to 160°C for 5 minutes. Lightly butter 8 muffin cases.

2. In a mixing bowl, thoroughly combine the flour, salt, vanilla, and cinnamon.

3. In a separate mixing bowl, beat the eggs

until frothy. Now, mash the berries and add them to the beaten eggs. Stir in the sugar and butter, and beat until everything is well combined.

4. Slowly and gradually, add the dry ingredients to the wet ingredients. Spoon the batter into the prepared muffin cases. Place 4 muffin cases in each drawer.

5. Select zone 1 and pair it with "BAKE" at 160°C for 15 minutes. Select "MATCH" followed by the "START/STOP" button.

6. Check the muffins for doneness and let them sit on a cooling rack for about 10 minutes before unmolding and serving.

7. Meanwhile, make the buttercream: Beat the sifted icing sugar with butter, gradually adding 2 to 3 tablespoons of hot water, until creamy, uniform, and smooth.

8. Add vanilla and mix to combine. Decorate your cupcakes with buttercream and enjoy!

Pumpkin Pie

Serves 8

Prep time: 10 minutes / Cook time: 19 minutes

Ingredients
- 500 g Pie Crust
- 500 g Instant Pot Pumpkin Pie Filling

Preparation instructions:

1. Make your pumpkin pie filling first, then proceed. Always do this first so that I can prepare the pie crust while the pressure cooks. Approximately 500g of cubed pumpkin is all that is needed to make a medium-sized pie.

2. While it is under pressure, prepare your pie crust. After mixing the lard into the flour, sugar, and mixture, add the water gradually until the dough is pliable enough to form a pie crust.

3. To make your cake pan non-stick, spray it

with extra virgin olive oil and massage it in with your hands.

4. After that, cover the cake pan with the pumpkin pie dough you just rolled out on a clean work surface dusted with flour. Edges should be cut. Mix your pumpkin pie filling and then pour it over your pie crust when the instant pot beeps.

5. Place the raw pumpkin pie in the air fryer, then cook it for an additional 5 minutes at 160°C after 12 minutes at 170°C .

6. If you have extra pie dough and filling, roll part of it out and cut it into small pies.

7. Then load into the air fryer and cook for 12 minutes at 170°C.

Bread And Butter Pudding

Serves 5

Prep time: 5 minutes / Cook time: 10 minutes

Ingredients
- 4 Slices Stale Thick Sliced Bread
- 1 Tsp Vanilla Essence
- 120 ml Semi Skimmed Milk
- 240 ml Raisins
- 2 Tbsp Butter
- 3 Large Eggs
- 240 ml Double Cream
- 80 ml Caster Sugar
- 1 Tsp Cinnamon
- Extra Virgin Olive Oil Spray
- Icing Sugar optional

Preparation Instructions :

1. Crack the eggs into a bowl, then add the cream, sugar, vanilla, and cinnamon. Blend with a fork.

2. Cut your bread into thick slices.

3. The bread should be completely coated in the batter once you've fully mixed the ingredients.

4. Your air fryer will be prepared by being drizzled with extra virgin olive oil and then being sprinkled with a pastry brush.
5. Fill the air fryer with batter-soaked bread, leaving any little pieces that would break up inside, and cook for 5 minutes at 190°C.
6. Place the bread in the bowl with the little pieces, then stir in the milk and raisins.
7. Put the bowl's contents in a container that is appropriate for air frying, and then sprinkle some butter on top. At 200°C, air fried for an additional 5 minutes. Before serving, add some icing sugar.

Scottish Smoked Salmon Bake

Serves 4

Prep time: 6 minutes / Cook time: 15 minutes

Ingredients

- 250g smoked salmon chunks
- 80g smoked salmon shavings
- 100g soft cheese
- 4 eggs, beaten
- 220ml milk
- 20g fresh parsley, chopped
- 20g chives, finely diced
- 10g spring onions, finely diced
- 1/8 tsp ground pepper
- 1Cal olive fry spray

Preparation Instructions

1. Preheat the dual zone to 180°C for 5 minutes
2. Spray two 4" bake pots, then place the salmon chunks in
3. Employing another medium sized bowl, toss in soft cheese and beat it with a fork
4. Add egg and milk to form a mixture, then top with chives, parsley, and spring onions
5. Toss this newly formed mixture on top of the salmon chunks
6. Top the pots with the salmon shavings

7. Place the baking pots in the draws of the dual zone and pairing them to 'BAKE' at 180°C for 15 minutes
8. Retrieve the fish bake, divide each bake pot into 2 servings

Traditional Steak and Kidney Pie

Serves 8-10

Prep time: 5 minutes / Cook time: 15 minutes

Ingredients

- 1 kg steak and kidney filler
- 4 sheet puff pastry
- 1cal olive oil fry spray
- 2 eggs, beaten

Preparation Instructions

1. Preheat the dual zone to 180° for 6 minutes
2. Meanwhile, cut out 4x6" baking tin shaped pastry's
3. Spray 2 x 6" baking tins thoroughly using the fry spray
4. Fill the ramekins with a layer of pastry then tip with the filling and cover with another layer of pastry
5. Make a small incisions at the centre of the pastries
6. Brush over the top of the pastries with the beaten egg
7. Place a pie in each draw of the dual zone and pair them to 'BAKE' at 180°C for 12-15 minutes
8. Once done, retrieve the steak and cut each pie into 4-5 slices to serve

Zesty Lemon Cake Pots

Serves 2

Prep time: 5 minutes / Cook time: 4 minutes

Ingredients

- Cake Ingredients
- 18g blanched almonds
- 15g high-fibre coconut flour
- ½ tsp baking soda
- 1 large pinch of xanthan gum
- 30g unsalted butter
- 1 egg
- 1 tsp sugar
- 1 tsp lemon juice
- 1 tsp lemon zest
- Garnish
- 30g lemon curd
- 20g lemon sherbet sauce

Preparation Instructions

1. Using a small bowl, stir together the almonds, sugar coconut flour, baking soda, lemon zest and xanthan gum
2. Employing a stand mixer, amalgamate butter, egg and lemon juice using a stand
3. Combine these wet and dry mixtures and fold the Ingredients
4. Pour this rich mixture into 2 small baking pots and place them in the ninja foodie zones
5. Select the zones and pair them with 'BAKE' for 4 minutes at 180°C
6. Press 'MATCH' followed by 'START/STOP' to bake
7. Retrieve the cake and brush with lemon curd and drizzle the lemon sherbet sauce, then serve

Fruit Bake Duo

Serves 6

Prep time: 6 minutes / Cook time: 13 minutes

Ingredients

- 2 large sheet of puff pasty
- 1 Pineapple
- 2 Large pink lady Apples
- 75g brown sugar
- 60g melted butter
- 2 tsp ground cinnamon

Preparation Instructions

1. Using a sharp knife, remove the skin and seeds from the Pineapple, the peel the apples
2. Cut the pineapple and apples and horizontally (6 pineapple slices and 6 apple slices)
3. Using a biscuit cutter, extract the core from the Pineapple and the apples to create fruit rings, then put them aside
4. Slice both sheets of puff pastry into long thin strips
5. Wrap the puff pastry strips around each fruit ring until the flesh is no longer visible (wrap under the centre cavity and around)
6. Brush over the pastries with the melted butter
7. Drizzle and massage the brown sugar and cinnamon on the fruit pastries
8. Using some kitchen tongs, place the pineapple pastries into the zone 1 draw and apple pastries into the zone 2 draw
9. Select the zones, using the 'BAKE' function at 190°C for 13 minutes
10. Press 'MATCH' then 'START/STOP' to cook the pastries
11. Using some kitchen tongs, plate the caramelised fruit ring bakes, then serve

Sweet & Sour Chicken Balls

Serves 2

Prep time: 6 minutes / Cook time: 12 minutes

Ingredients

- Frozen Chicken Balls
- Frozen Sweet & Sour Sauce
- 1 Tsp Extra Virgin Olive Oil

Preparation Instructions

1. Load frozen sweet and sour chicken balls into the air fryer basket.
2. Cook for 8 minutes at a temperature of 180°C Shake the air fryer chicken balls and place the sweet and sour sachet in the air fryer too.
3. Spray a little olive oil onto your chicken balls. Cook for a further 4 minutes at 200°C to help make your chicken balls crispier.
4. Serve with your sweet and sour sauce.

Easy Cinnamon Pear Cake

Serves: 8 slices

Prep time: 15 minutes / Cook time: 25-30 minutes

Ingredients

- 240 g all-purpose flour
- 200g caster sugar
- 1 teaspoon of baking powder
- 170 g of cold margarine
- 1 large or 2 medium eggs
- 120 ml whole milk

For the Topping:
- 4 tablespoons of caster sugar
- 2 tablespoons of cinnamon
- 3 large ripe pears or 4 to 5 smaller ripe pears

Preparation Instructions

1. Preheat your air fryer to 200°C and grease the cake pan attachment.
2. Combine the flour, sugar, baking powder and all of the margarine in a large mixing bowl. I suggest mixing with a fork. Make sure your margarine is cold during this process and mix until the ingredients reassemble a fine breadcrumb mixture.
3. Whisk the egg(s) thoroughly and add to the mixture along with the milk. Stir until creamy but not firm.
4. Add the rest of the sugar and flour and stir.
5. Place the completed mixture into your greased cake pan.
6. Top and tail your pears, and then cut into quarters. Afterwards, slice the pears thinly and arrange them in a fan shape across the cake.
7. Combine your cinnamon and sugar, then sprinkle over the top of your pears. Bake for 30 minutes in your air fryer or until a knife comes out of the cake cleanly.

Printed in Great Britain
by Amazon

22566199R00053